THE Make it Simple! COOKBOOK

For information about the Weight Watchers classes,
contact:
Weight Watchers UK Limited
11 Fairacres
Dedworth Road
Windsor
Berkshire SL4 4UY
Telephone: (0753) 856751

Art Director: Roger Judd
Designer: Jeremy Dixon
Photography: Simon Smith at Barry Bullough's Studio
Line Drawings: David Clark
Food prepared by Ann Page-Wood
Stylist: Kathy Man

British Library Cataloguing in Publication Data

The Make it Simple! cookbook.
  1. Reducing diets —— Recipes
  I. Weight Watchers
  641.5'635   TX837
  ISBN 0-450-41571-6

First published in Great Britain in 1987 by New English Library,
Mill Road, Dunton Green, Sevenoaks, Kent, a division of
Hodder & Stoughton Limited

Photoset by Rowland Phototypesetting Limited,
Bury St Edmunds, Suffolk
Printed and bound by Hazell, Watson & Viney Limited,
a member of the BPCC group of companies,
Aylesbury, Bucks

THE Make it Simple! COOKBOOK

Weight Watchers *

step-by-step guide to easy cooking with
Ann Page-Wood

NEW ENGLISH LIBRARY

INTRODUCTION

How many times have we started a slimming diet, determined to lose those unwanted pounds, only to give it up when the lure of a favourite nibble becomes impossible to ignore? It's easy to become bored and frustrated when the first burst of enthusiasm wears off, especially when we're forbidden to eat the foods we crave. But with the wealth of delicious foods available today, it's possible to enjoy a satisfying, varied diet and still lose weight! In *The Make it Simple! Cookbook* we show you how.

The introduction to each section contains detailed descriptions and easy-to-follow instructions, with illustrations, to help you choose, prepare and cook the ingredients in a healthy and imaginative way. Why not add a few herbs when you're baking fish or serve an unusual salad or stir-fry instead of boring boiled vegetables?

Every one of the mouthwatering recipes has been tested and we provide straightforward, step-by-step instructions to help you achieve the best results. We also include calorie counts. Weight Watchers members please note that all the recipes in this book have been based on the Weight Watchers Quick Start Plus Food Plan and Programme Exchanges are given with each recipe.

Measurements are given in imperial and metric (never mix the two in the same recipe) and quantities are generally given for two people, although it's easy to double or treble them to feed the family or guests.

Take care when you're shopping for fresh ingredients. When you can, make use of self-service greengrocers and supermarkets where you can pick the best quality produce and buy exactly the quantity you wish – as little as 2oz (60g) of mushrooms if that's all the recipe requires. In this way you won't be tempted to eat leftover ingredients. If a recipe calls for half a green pepper, you can store the other half in an open polythene bag in the refrigerator and use it within a few days.

CONTENTS

POINTS TO NOTE

Ingredients

Eggs
All recipes requiring eggs have been tested with size 3 eggs. Don't use any other size.

Fats and Oils
The margarine and oils are always those high in polyunsaturated fats. Look carefully for this on the labels. When a recipe lists 'vegetable oil', oils such as corn, sunflower, safflower, soybean or peanut may be used. As olive oil has such a strong flavour it is specified when suitable. As the margarines high in polyunsaturated fats are very soft, it is worthwhile freezing a quantity for use in the 'rubbing in' method of recipes. To reduce the amount of fat used in cooking and therefore reduce the number of calories, it is worth lining baking sheets and tins with non-stick baking parchment instead of greasing them. This will also make washing up easier.

Fruit
Unless specified, fresh fruit has been used but frozen or canned fruit packed in natural juice with no added sugar may be substituted when appropriate. However this may alter the cooking time and consistency of a dish.

Meat and Poultry
Always buy the leanest possible meat. It is often best to buy meat, remove any visible fat and mince it yourself to save buying fatty minced meat. Meat and poultry skin should be removed, whenever possible, before cooking. Cook all meat, except offal and poultry, on a rack under the grill, or bake in the oven for a few minutes, turning once until fat has stopped dripping from the cut before proceeding with any recipe. Alternatively, boil the meat for a short time, allow to cool then skim off the fat. Always bake or roast meat on a rack and never use the fat that runs out in gravies, sauces etc. All the weights of meat given in the list of ingredients are for the uncooked meat trimmed of all fat. As meat shrinks during cooking, weigh after cooking. About 4oz (120g) uncooked meat weighs 3oz (90g) when cooked.

Milk
Always use fresh or long life skimmed milk or reconstituted skimmed milk powder.

Seasonings
The herbs used in the recipes are dried unless otherwise indicated. If you wish to substitute fresh herbs, use about three times the quantity of dried. Herbs and spices lose their flavour during storage. If possible store in a dark cupboard and never keep longer than a year. Whenever pepper is used, freshly ground black pepper is recommended.

Vegetables
Unless otherwise indicated, fresh vegetables have been used but

frozen or canned may be
substituted when appropriate.
However, remember this may alter
the cooking time and consistency of
a dish.

Weighing

Accuracy is vital to achieve good
results when cooking and to help
control your own weight. Measure
ingredients carefully and use only
one system; the imperial or the
metric. Always use accurate spoon
measures: 1 teaspoon is equivalent
to 5ml and 1 tablespoon is
equivalent to 15ml. An approximate
conversion table is given below:

Liquids

½fl oz (1 tablespoon)	15ml
1fl oz	30ml
2fl oz	60ml
3fl oz	90ml
4fl oz	120ml
5fl oz (¼ pint)	150ml
6fl oz	180ml
7fl oz	210ml
8fl oz	240ml
9fl oz	270ml
10fl oz (½ pint)	300ml
11fl oz	330ml
12fl oz	360ml
13fl oz	390ml
14fl oz	420ml
15fl oz (¾ pint)	450ml
16fl oz	480ml
20fl oz (1 pint)	600ml
35fl oz	1 litre
40fl oz (2 pints)	1 litre 200ml

Solids

½oz	15g
1oz	30g
2oz	60g
3oz	90g
4oz	120g
5oz	150g
6oz	180g
7oz	210g
8oz	240g
9oz	270g
10oz	300g
11oz	330g
12oz	360g
13oz	390g
14oz	420g
15oz	450g
1lb	480g

EGGS AND CHEESE

Eggs

Eggs are probably the most versatile ingredient in the kitchen. They supply essential proteins, vitamins and minerals and can be cooked and served on their own, used to enrich a variety of mixtures, bind foods together, hold air in cakes and soufflés and be used to thicken or set sauces and custards. A beaten egg added to a basic bread dough makes a softer textured, richer bread.

The term 'egg' is used for eggs of all domestic fowl. All the recipes in this book use the standard size 3 egg. The colour of the shell, whether brown or white, does not indicate any difference in food value or freshness. They are simply produced by different breeds of hen. Other eggs such as quail or duck eggs are always labelled according to their origin. It's important to note the difference between free-range eggs and barn or perchery eggs, which many people buy believing them to be free-range. Legally, free-range hens must have continual daytime access to open-air runs, their buildings must have litter material on at least a third of the floor, and each hen must have at least 10 square metres of floor space. On the other hand, there may be as many as 25 barn or perchery hens per square metre of floor space, and each hen has a perch space of about 15 centimetres.

How to tell an egg is fresh

Dissolve a tablespoon of salt in half a pint (300ml) of cold water and place the egg in the water. A very fresh egg will lay on its side on the bottom, a less fresh egg will stand on one end and a very stale egg will float.

Another test is to break the egg onto a plate. A very fresh egg will have three distinct components: the yolk which should be domed, the thick white which surrounds the yolk and a border of thin white which surrounds that. As an egg ages, the yolk flattens and the white becomes thinner, making it harder to distinguish between the thick and thin layers. The short white chalazae, which looks like a white string attached to the yolk, doesn't indicate freshness but plays an important part in keeping an egg fresh.

Fresh eggs take less time to cook and hold more air when whisked than older eggs.

How to store eggs

Always store eggs in a cool place with the pointed end down so the chalazae is able to suspend the yolk in the centre of the white. If kept in the refrigerator, keep well away from the ice box and allow the egg to return to room temperature before use. This will help to reduce the risk of the shell cracking when boiling and enable it to hold more air if it is to be whisked. Keep eggs well away from foods with strong smells such as fish or cheese as they will absorb the smell.

The properties of eggs

Egg white sets at about 71°C (150°F) whereas the yolk coagulates at

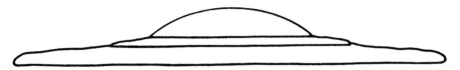

A very fresh egg with three distinct components:
the yolk, thick white and thin white.

approximately 75°C (160°F), well below boiling point. If heated above their coagulating temperature the proteins in the egg white and yolk become increasingly tough and shrink. An egg can be poached in simmering water so the white sets but the yolk remains runny. When eggs are used to thicken a stirred custard it's important to stir continuously, using a double saucepan or in a bowl standing over a saucepan of simmering water, otherwise the white will set before the yolk has thickened the custard. The importance of carefully controlling the cooking temperature is easily seen when making a baked egg custard. The custard is cooked when it reaches the consistency of a jelly. A knife should be inserted through the skin and each side of the cut gently pressed. If no liquid oozes out, the custard is set. If cooking is continued, the proteins will toughen, shrink and squeeze the water out of the custard causing it to separate or 'curdle' and turn from a jelly-like consistency to a hard tough custard surrounded by water. To prevent overheating it is advisable to stand the custard in a water bath and never bake over Gas Mark 3, 160°C, 325°F.

The thickening ability of eggs is used to bind various ingredients together, for example when making a stuffing. Their property of setting at a low temperature is used when foods are coated in beaten egg and rolled in breadcrumbs before dotting with fat and baking or frying. The egg sets, preventing the food from absorbing fat but enabling the outer coating to form a crunchy, golden brown crust. Pastries and breads are sometimes brushed with beaten egg to give the food an appealing golden brown colour after cooking.

The yolk, and to a far greater extent the white, have the ability to hold air. Beaten whole eggs are gradually incorporated into creamed cake mixtures to lighten the cake and help it rise. In whisked cake mixtures the only raising agent is the egg. Eggs are whisked with about half their weight of caster sugar in a bowl standing over a saucepan of simmering water until the mixture changes to a pale creamy colour, increases considerably in bulk and thickens. Then sifted plain flour and/or other ingredients are folded in before baking. Egg whites are particularly useful in whisked mixtures and are folded into soufflés, mousses etc. to act as the raising agent. A pinch of salt or cream of tartar helps the egg white to hold air as it creates a more stable foam.

It is worth noting that once an egg white has been whisked to a foam, if put to one side the foam will gradually break down and liquify. It won't be able to be rewhisked as the structure of the egg white will have been altered.

The egg white is important as it plays the greatest part in trapping air into a mixture, but the egg yolk is able to hold fat in emulsion. Eggs, when beaten into a creamed cake mixture, help the mixture to remain light and of an even consistency and prevent curdling. They're especially useful when making mayonnaise. One egg yolk is able to hold ¼ pint (150ml) of oil suspended in emulsion.

Cooking with eggs

Boiled Eggs: To achieve the desired result – soft-boiled, just firm or hard-boiled – takes practice, and the saying, 'He can't even boil an egg' seems rather unfair as boiling an egg perfectly is not easy. Soft-boiled eggs can be cooked either by being placed in simmering water and cooking for 3½–4 minutes or by covering with cold water, bringing to the boil, reducing the heat and simmering for 1 minute. Hard-boiled eggs should be lowered into boiling water, then simmered for 10–11 minutes. To prevent a black line of discolouration around the yolk, plunge the eggs immediately into cold water and remove the shell.

Coddled Eggs: To obtain a lightly set coddled egg, place the egg in a greased china or glass coddler or leave in its shell and stand in sufficient boiling water to just cover it. Cover the saucepan, remove from the heat, leave for 8–10 minutes, then serve.

Poached Eggs: It isn't necessary to buy an egg poacher. Half fill a small frying pan with water, add a few drops of vinegar or a little salt (this will help to prevent the egg white spreading) and bring to the boil. Break the egg into a damp cup, then slide it into the boiling water. Reduce the heat and simmer until the white sets, 2½–3 minutes. Remove the egg with a fish slice. If you prefer a more evenly shaped egg, lightly grease a pastry cutter, place in the frying pan and slide the egg into the cutter to cook.

Baked Eggs: Lightly grease small individual ramekins and warm in the oven. Break an egg into each dish, season with salt and pepper and bake at Gas Mark 4, 180°C, 350°F, for 6–8 minutes or until just set.

Scrambled Eggs: Heat a little margarine in a small saucepan. Lightly whisk an egg with a tablespoon of water or milk, season with salt and pepper. Pour the egg into the saucepan and cook over a low heat, stirring all the time, until the egg thickens and sets. Take great care not to overcook the egg or it will lose its creamy texture and become tough with a watery liquid.

Fried Eggs: Heat a little margarine or oil in a frying pan until hot, add the broken egg and, using a teaspoon, spoon over the hot fat to baste the top of the egg and enable it to cook evenly. Remove from the pan with a fish slice.

Cheese

What is cheese?
Cheese making was originally a method of preserving milk when it was plentiful for times when it became scarce, but it's long been recognised as a valuable food in its own right. Basically a solidified form of milk, cheese is rich in protein and minerals and, according to the type of cheese, may provide a considerable amount of fat.

There are hundreds of different cheeses – France alone claims to produce over four hundred varieties – but in this book they are divided into two basic categories: hard, processed and soft cheeses, and low-fat, cottage and curd cheeses and cheese spreads.

Hard, processed and soft cheeses
This category includes any of the above cheeses up to the calorific value of 120 calories per ounce (30g). There are a few which are higher in calories, for example, Blue Stilton.

The term 'lean' cheese refers to hard cheeses made from skimmed milk, for example Edam. 'Processed' cheese describes a hard cheese which has been mulled, mixed with milk to obtain a softer consistency, then pasteurised and wrapped before sale.

There are so many cheeses included in this category it would be impossible to name them all, but the following list gives a brief description of a few of them.

Austrian Smoked

This is usually sold in a sausage shape or small round. It has a brown skin containing the pale soft textured cheese. It has a mild smoky flavour and is best suited to uncooked recipes such as salads.

Blue Vinney

A traditional British hard cheese made from skimmed cows' milk. It has a fairly hard texture, is white in colour with blue veining and a strong flavour.

Bel Paese

An Italian hard cheese made from whole milk. It is a rich cheese with a slightly rubbery texture and mild flavour.

Boursin

A soft creamy textured cheese from France, pale in colour and made from whole milk.

Brie

A flat, soft textured French cheese made from whole milk. It should be a very pale yellow and the texture creamy, not runny. It doesn't keep well so eat within a few days of purchase.

Caerphilly

Originally made in Wales, this is a fairly hard but soft textured cheese, mild in flavour and best served uncooked. It is made from whole milk and is lightly pressed and sold when about ten days old.

Camembert

A round, soft, flat French cheese made from whole milk. The cheese should be a very pale yellow and smooth textured without holes. It has a distinct flavour.

Cheddar

Probably the most well known cheese. It was originally made in Somerset from whole milk but is now produced in many parts of the British Isles as well as Canada, New Zealand and Australia. The name is now used to describe cheese which is made by the Cheddar process. The flavour and colour varies from very mild to mature and strong, and from pale yellow to a rich yellow colour.

Cheshire

A traditional whole milk British cheese. There are two types: the white and the artificially coloured red. Occasionally the red cheese develops a blue veining. The cheese has a fairly crumbly texture and a mild mellow flavour. It is widely used in cooking when a strong flavour is not required.

Danish Blue

A Danish cheese which has a white crumbly texture and a blue veining. It has a sharp, slightly salty flavour.

Derby

A traditional British cheese made from whole milk. It has a close texture and the young cheeses have a mild flavour which develops as it matures. Sage leaves are sometimes layered in the curd to produce Sage Derby which has green bands across the cheese and a sage flavour.

Edam

A Dutch 'lean' cheese made from skimmed milk. It is ball shaped and covered with a bright red waxy coating. The cheese is yellow in colour with a mild flavour and smooth texture.

Emmenthal

A Swiss hard cheese usually made from whole milk. It is pale yellow in colour and the texture is smooth with many holes or 'eyes'. It has a straw-coloured rind.

Gloucester

A British hard cheese. Traditionally the cheese was made from either morning milk, which has a lower fat content than other milk, or skimmed evening milk. There are two types of Gloucester cheese: Single and Double. Both have strong mellow flavours but the Single Gloucester has a slightly soft, open texture whereas the Double Gloucester is more crumbly.

Gorgonzola

A soft Italian cheese with blue veining. It has a distinctive sharp flavour.

Lancashire

A British, fairly hard cheese made from whole milk. It has a slightly crumbly texture and a mild flavour which develops as the cheese matures. It is a good quality cheese for cooking.

Leicester

A traditional British hard cheese made from whole milk. It is an orange-red colour and has a mild flavour.

Lymeswold

This is a fairly recently produced British cheese similar to the French Blue Brie and the German Cambozola. It isn't a traditional cheese and isn't named after the place of production.

Mozzarella

An Italian soft cheese originally made from buffalo milk but now usually made from cows' milk. It must be used when fresh. It is very pale in colour, egg-shaped and dripping with buttermilk. Rarely eaten raw, it's usually incorporated in Italian recipes such as pizzas, lasagnes, etc.

Parmesan

The hardest Italian cheese which is made from skimmed milk and may be matured for as long as 2–4 years. It has a very strong distinctive flavour and must be finely grated before adding to dishes. It is pale yellow in colour with very tiny holes, the size of a pin prick, and an almost black crust. It is well worth buying fresh Parmesan and grating it for use in recipes. The tubs of ready grated Parmesan are not so strongly flavoured.

Roquefort

A traditional French cheese made from ewes' milk. The curds of the cheese are mixed with dried breadcrumbs which are ground finely and left to develop a particular greenish mould. A good Roquefort should have a grey rind and be a pale yellow colour with even blue veining.

Wensleydale   The original British Wensleydale was a double cream cheese with a blue vein. Nowadays it isn't ripened and is sold when a mild creamy colour with a crumbly texture.

Low-fat, cottage and curd cheeses and cheese spreads

This category of cheeses includes low-fat cottage and curd cheeses and cheese spreads up to the calorific value of 50 calories per ounce (30g). The majority of these types of cheese have their calorific value on their packaging and it is worth checking.

The low-fat cheeses such as quark, cottage and curd cheese are usually made from either skimmed or semi-skimmed milk which has rennet added to it or is soured to form curds and whey. The curds are broken up to form cottage cheese and left as a smooth consistency for curd cheese. I prefer curd cheese for use in cooking as it gives a better flavour.

I don't propose to explain the production and uses of cheese spreads in cooking as they are best used, as their name implies, as spreads but they may be incorporated into dips or other simple recipes.

How to store cheese

Although it may take several years to produce a well-matured cheese, once cut and removed from the carefully controlled atmosphere in which it was stored it will deteriorate remarkably quickly. Soft cheeses lose their flavour within a few days, but hard cheeses can be stored for much longer. Wrap the cheese loosely, preferably with waxed paper, cover and store in a cool place. Do not store in an airtight container. If the only available cool place is the refrigerator, follow the same rules and remember to remove the cheese at least an hour before serving to enjoy the flavour at its best.

How to cook cheese

It is often said that hard cheese is difficult to digest due to the fat surrounding the protein. In order to aid the digestion, it is advisable to eat it with a starchy food or to grate it before incorporating into a salad so it is already in small pieces before entering the mouth. To increase the savoury flavour of cheese, add a little mustard to recipes for cheese sauces or to a salad dressing which is to be served with a cheese salad. Never overcook cheese or it will become tough; cook it for the shortest possible time. For example, when making a cheese sauce: make a white sauce, boil it, reduce the heat and stir in the grated cheese. When grilling a dish covered with cheese sauce, sprinkle the sauce with a few fresh breadcrumbs. These will absorb some of the fat and give a crisp coating. Never keep a cheese dish hot for more than a few minutes.

SPANISH OMELETTE
Serves 1 (335 Calories per serving)

This is a meal in itself. Use a non-stick or heavy-based omelette pan, as the omelette is turned to cook the underside and not folded over. You may find it easier to slide the omelette onto a plate, then invert it back into the pan.

I teaspoon olive or vegetable oil
¼ green pepper, cored and chopped
¼ red pepper, cored and chopped
I shallot or ½ small onion, chopped
I small tomato, peeled and chopped
3oz (90g) cooked potato, diced
I oz (30g) cooked peas
2 eggs, beaten
2 tablespoons water
good pinch mixed herbs
salt and pepper

① Heat the oil in a 7½-inch (19-cm) omelette pan. Add the peppers and onion and stir-fry for about 4 minutes or until soft. Add the tomato, potato and peas.

② In a bowl whisk together all the remaining ingredients.

③ Pour the egg mixture over the vegetables, stir round and cook over a moderate heat, shaking the pan occasionally and easing the edge of the omelette away from the pan.

④ When the underside is golden brown, slide onto a plate using a fish slice. Turn upside down back into the pan and continue cooking until the other side is golden brown.

⑤ Slide the thick omelette onto a warm serving plate.

Exchanges per serving:
Bread 1
Fat 1
Protein 2
Vegetable 2

Spanish Omelette

SPINACH OMELETTE
Serves 1 (330 Calories per serving)

Omelettes are very easy to make. Cook them over a moderate heat while drawing the mixture in with a fork so the base sets and turns golden brown but the top remains a creamy consistency.

2 eggs
1 tablespoon water
salt and pepper
3oz (90g) spinach, roughly chopped
1 teaspoon margarine
1 tablespoon single cream
1 tablespoon grated Parmesan cheese
freshly grated nutmeg

① Beat the eggs with the water, salt and pepper.

② Thoroughly wash the spinach, place in a saucepan, cover and cook gently.

③ Heat the margarine in a 6–7-inch (15–18-cm) omelette pan and when bubbling, pour in the egg mixture and switch on the heat under the spinach.

④ Draw the egg mixture from the sides of the pan into the centre using the prongs of a fork or a spatula until the egg sets. Continue cooking over a moderate heat until the underside is golden brown.

⑤ Drain any excess water from the spinach, stir in the single cream and 2 teaspoons Parmesan cheese, season with salt, pepper and nutmeg.

⑥ Place the spinach on one half of the omelette, fold the other half over to form a semi-circle. Transfer to a warm serving plate and sprinkle over the remaining Parmesan cheese.

> *Exchanges per serving:*
> Fat 1
> Protein 2
> Vegetable 1
> 65 Calories Optional Exchange

PEPPER FRITTATA
Serves I (345 Calories per serving)

A frittata is cooked very slowly over a low heat, the opposite method to cooking an omelette, and when the base is golden brown the pan is transferred to a grill to complete the cooking. It is served whole, not folded over. A crisp salad makes an ideal accompaniment.

1 ½ teaspoons vegetable or olive oil
1 small clove garlic, finely chopped
1 tablespoon chopped spring onion
¼ green pepper, cored and chopped
¼ red pepper, cored and chopped
2 eggs
2 tablespoons water
1 oz (30g) Double Gloucester, finely grated (or a mixture of Double Gloucester and Parmesan or Cheddar)
salt and pepper

① Heat ½ teaspoon of oil in a 7-inch (18-cm) omelette pan. Add the garlic, onion and peppers and stir-fry 4–5 minutes until soft.

② Beat the eggs and water together in a bowl, add the stir-fried vegetables, about half the cheese and salt and pepper.

③ Add the remaining oil to the omelette pan, heat over a low heat, swirl round the pan.

④ Pour the egg mixture into the pan, turn the heat down to low and cook very slowly without stirring for 10–12 minutes until the underside is golden. Remove from the heat, sprinkle with the remaining cheese.

⑤ Transfer to a preheated grill and cook until the cheese has melted and is bubbling. Slide onto a warm serving plate.

Exchanges per serving:
Fat 1 ½
Protein 3
Vegetable 1

BROCCOLI AU GRATIN
Serves 2 (415 Calories per serving)

This recipe can be adapted to use with a wide variety of vegetables according to what is economical and in season. Try substituting the broccoli with halved small leeks.

10oz (300g) calabrese broccoli	½ pint (300ml) skimmed milk
salt	2oz (60g) strong-flavoured hard cheese, grated
3oz (90g) thinly sliced smoked ham	
For the sauce	salt and pepper
4 teaspoons margarine	*For the topping and garnish*
¾oz (20g) flour	¼oz (10g) fresh breadcrumbs
good pinch powdered mustard	1 tomato

① Cut the broccoli into even-sized pieces. Boil in salted water until just cooked but still crisp, 8–10 minutes, drain well and wrap the slices of ham round the stems of the broccoli, cutting the slices in half if necessary.

② While the broccoli is boiling, make the sauce. Melt the margarine over a low heat, add the flour and stir over the heat for 1 minute.

③ Gradually add the powdered mustard and milk.

④ Bring the sauce to the boil, stirring all the time, reduce the heat and simmer for about 3 minutes.

Reserve a tablespoon of the cheese, stir the remainder into the sauce and season well with salt and pepper.

⑤ Arrange the hot broccoli and ham in a flameproof dish. Pour over the cheese sauce and sprinkle with the reserved cheese and breadcrumbs. Place under a preheated grill until the top begins to brown.

⑥ Remove from the heat, arrange slices or wedges of tomato around the dish and return to the grill until the cheese is bubbling and the tomato heated through.

Exchanges per serving:
Bread ½
Fat 2
Milk ½
Protein 2½
Vegetable 2

STUFFED EGGS
Serves 2 (230 Calories per serving)

This is a simple, basic recipe which you can adapt to suit your own taste and ring the changes. Try adding a little minced cooked ham or flaked tuna to the stuffing, and serve them on a bed of shredded lettuce.

4 hard-boiled eggs, shelled
I tablespoon low-calorie mayonnaise
2 teaspoons chopped chives
½ teaspoon anchovy essence
2oz (60g) cottage or low-fat soft cheese
salt
paprika
sprigs of parsley to garnish

① Halve the eggs lengthways and scoop out the yolks into a bowl.

② Mash the egg yolks with the mayonnaise, chives, anchovy essence and cottage cheese. Season with a little salt.

③ Either pile the stuffing back into the egg whites or place in a piping bag fitted with a ½-inch (1.25-cm) star nozzle and pipe into the whites.

④ Dust each egg with a little paprika and garnish with sprigs of parsley.

Exchanges per serving:
Fat ¾
Protein 2½

SPINACH AND EGG RAMEKINS
Serves 2 (240 Calories per serving)

This is a useful recipe which can be made up from ingredients out of the freezer or storecupboard.

½ teaspoon margarine
12oz (360g) frozen chopped spinach
2 eggs
8 teaspoons single cream
salt and pepper
1oz (30g) Cheddar cheese, grated

① Grease two 4-inch (10-cm) ramekins or ovenproof dishes.

② Boil the spinach according to the instructions, press in a sieve to drain really well.

③ Divide the spinach between the two ramekins, make a deep well in the centre. Break an egg into each well.

④ Spoon 4 teaspoons of cream over each egg and season well with salt and pepper.

⑤ Bake at Gas Mark 4, 180°C, 350°F for 20 minutes. Remove from the oven, sprinkle with the cheese and grill for 1–2 minutes until the cheese is bubbling and just beginning to brown.

Exchanges per serving:
Fat ¼
Protein 1½
Vegetable 2
45 Calories Optional Exchange

CHEESE SOUFFLÉ
Serves 2 (435 Calories per serving)

This is a basic soufflé recipe. The cheese may be omitted and replaced with 2oz (60g) finely chopped ham or a mixture of cheese and ham. Don't be tempted to add too much filling or the soufflé will be heavy. Always serve soufflés immediately – the minute they are removed from the oven they begin to sink.

4 teaspoons margarine
½oz (15g) flour
¼ pint (150ml) skimmed milk
3 eggs, separated
1½oz (45g) Cheddar cheese, grated
1½oz (45g) Parmesan cheese, grated
1 tablespoon chopped chives or spring onions
salt and pepper
good pinch powdered mustard

① Use a little of the margarine to grease a 6-inch (15-cm) soufflé dish.

② Heat the remaining margarine in a 2-pint (1-litre 200-ml) saucepan, add the flour and cook over a low heat for 1–2 minutes, stirring all the time.

③ Remove from the heat and gradually blend in the milk. Bring to the boil, stirring continuously, boil for 1 minute.

④ Allow to cool a little then beat in the egg yolks, cheeses and chives, season to taste with salt, pepper and mustard.

⑤ Whisk the egg whites with a pinch of salt until peaking. Lightly fold them into the cheese sauce using a tablespoon. Transfer the mixture to the soufflé dish and bake at Gas Mark 4, 180°C, 350°F for about 35 minutes until golden brown, well risen and just set. Serve immediately.

Exchanges per serving:
Bread ¼
Fat 2
Milk ¼
Protein 3

CREAMY TAGLIATELLE
Serves 2 (350 Calories per serving)

I prefer this recipe made with either verdi tagliatelle or a mixture of plain and verdi. The carrots should still be crisp; don't overcook them.

2oz (60g) tagliatelle
2 teaspoons vegetable oil
I small onion, chopped
I carrot, cut in thin strips
2oz (60g) button mushrooms, sliced
4oz (120g) curd cheese
3 tablespoons single cream
3oz (90g) cooked ham, cut in thin strips

① Cook the tagliatelle in boiling water according to the packaging instructions.

② Meanwhile, prepare the other ingredients. Heat the oil, add the onion and carrot and sauté for 4 minutes. Stir in the mushrooms and stir-fry for a further minute.

③ Mash the curd cheese and cream together, stir into the vegetables.

④ Add the cooked ham, stir over a moderate heat.

⑤ Drain the tagliatelle well, add to the saucepan and stir round to heat all the ingredients together. Season well and serve.

Exchanges per serving:

Bread 1

Fat 1

Protein 2½

Vegetable 1½

50 Calories Optional Exchange

PASTA SPIRALS WITH TWO CHEESES

Serves 2 (335 Calories per serving)

This is an unusual pasta dish with a strong, but not overpowering, cheese flavour. Heat the curd cheese very gently so it melts slowly and doesn't burn.

2oz (60g) pasta spirals
1 teaspoon vegetable oil
2 spring onions, cut in ¾-inch (1.75-cm) diagonal slices
½ red pepper, cored and cut into thin strips
½ green pepper, cored and cut into thin strips
4oz (120g) curd or low-fat soft cheese
salt and pepper
2oz (60g) Gorgonzola, grated or broken into very small pieces
1 tablespoon chopped parsley

① Boil the pasta spirals according to the packaging instructions, drain.

② Heat the oil, add the spring onions and peppers and stir-fry 4–5 minutes.

③ Add the curd cheese and heat through very gently, stirring all the time. Season well with salt and pepper.

④ Stir in the pasta and Gorgonzola and heat through, stirring continuously. Serve garnished with the chopped parsley.

Exchanges per serving:
Bread 1
Fat ½
Protein 2
Vegetable ½

RASPBERRY SOUFFLÉ
Serves 2 (200 Calories per serving)

Try this recipe with different fruits: make a thick fruit purée with blackberries, strawberries, apples or gooseberries, then add the egg yolks and whisked egg whites as described below.

¼ teaspoon margarine
10oz (300g) raspberries
1 tablespoon water
2 tablespoons sugar
2 teaspoons cornflour
2 eggs, separated
salt

1. Grease a 6-inch (15-cm) soufflé dish with the margarine.

2. Gently heat the raspberries, water and sugar in a saucepan. Simmer and stir the fruit to break it up and form a purée.

3. Blend the cornflour to a paste with a little of the fruit purée, tip the cornflour paste back into the saucepan and bring to the boil, stirring continuously. Boil for 2 minutes, allow to cool a little.

4. Stir the egg yolks into the raspberry purée.

5. Whisk the egg whites with a pinch of salt until peaking. Gently fold into the purée with a metal spoon.

6. Spoon the mixture into the prepared soufflé dish and bake at Gas Mark 4, 180°C, 350°F for about 30 minutes until well risen and just set. Serve immediately.

Exchanges per serving:
Fruit 1
Protein 1
75 Calories Optional Exchange

CARAMEL CUSTARD

Serves 2 (255 Calories per serving)

The delicate smooth-textured custard can very easily be spoilt if it is overcooked. Take very great care not to let the water in the steamer boil and don't cook for too long or the custard will be tough.

For the caramel
4 tablespoons granulated sugar
4 tablespoons cold water
2 teaspoons hot water
For the custard
2 eggs
2 teaspoons caster sugar
¼ pint (150ml) skimmed milk
3 drops vanilla essence

① Prepare a steamer, cut two rounds of non-stick baking parchment to cover the tops of the custards.

② Gently heat the granulated sugar and cold water in a heavy-based small saucepan until the liquid turns golden brown. Do not stir the liquid during this time. Remove from the heat.

③ Add the hot water. This will make a noise as it combines with the caramel.

④ Hold a ¼-pint (150-ml) ungreased metal basin in oven gloves, quickly pour in half the caramel and turn the basin to coat. Repeat with the other basin.

⑤ Beat the eggs, sugar and a tablespoon of milk together.

⑥ Heat the remaining milk until steaming, stir into the egg mixture, add the vanilla essence then strain into the metal basins.

⑦ Lay the non-stick baking parchment on top of the custards. Transfer to the steamer and steam very gently, not allowing the water in the steamer to simmer, for about 12–15 minutes until set.

⑧ Remove the basins from the steamer and tilt them so the custard draws away from the sides. Turn upside down onto the two serving plates and when the caramel has run from the base of the tins, carefully remove and serve.

Exchanges per serving:
Milk ¼
Protein 1
140 Calories Optional Exchange

STUFFED MUSHROOMS
Serves 2 (230 Calories per serving)

Either serve these mushrooms as a snack for two or as a starter for four people. For special occasions, cut circles of bread, toast and spread thinly with margarine, then serve each mushroom on the toast.

4 large flat mushrooms
(total weight 5½–6oz/165–180g)
1 teaspoon margarine
1 shallot or ½ small onion, finely chopped
4oz (120g) corned beef, chopped
1oz (30g) fresh wholemeal breadcrumbs
1 egg, beaten
salt and pepper

① Remove and chop the stalks from the mushrooms.

② Melt the margarine over a low heat. Add the shallot and mushroom stalks and stir-fry 3–4 minutes.

③ Mix the corned beef and breadcrumbs with the shallot, mashing the mixture with a fork. Add the egg and season well with salt and pepper.

④ Place the four mushrooms, gill side uppermost, on a piece of ungreased foil lying on a baking sheet. Divide the stuffing between the four mushrooms and loosely fold the foil over to make a parcel.

⑤ Bake in a preheated oven, Gas Mark 5, 190°C, 375°F for 25 minutes.

Exchanges per serving:
Bread ½
Fat ½
Protein 2½
Vegetable 1

FRANKFURTER SALAD
Serves 2 (365 Calories per serving)

I prefer this salad made with a wholewheat pasta but ordinary or verdi pasta of a small shape may be used. Don't use a very strong-flavoured cheese or it will dominate the other flavours. I've used Edam but you could use any mild hard cheese.

2oz (60g) wholewheat wheat ear-shaped pasta
3oz (90g) frankfurters
2oz (60g) Edam cheese
4 stuffed olives, sliced
½ red pepper, cored and chopped
½ yellow pepper, cored and chopped
For the dressing:
2 teaspoons olive oil
2 tablespoons lemon juice
¼ teaspoon French mustard
salt and pepper
few radicchio or chicory leaves to serve

① Cook the pasta in boiling water according to the packaging instructions, drain.

② Cut the frankfurters into ½-inch (1.25-cm) diagonal slices.

③ Cut the cheese into ½-inch (1.25-cm) cubes.

④ Mix together the pasta, frankfurters, cheese, olives, red and yellow peppers.

⑤ Place all the dressing ingredients together in a small bowl and whisk to mix or place in a screw-top jar and shake well.

⑥ Pour the dressing over the salad and toss to coat.

⑦ Arrange the radicchio or chicory leaves round the edge of the serving plate or bowl. Pile the salad in the centre.

Exchanges per serving:
Bread 1
Fat 1
Protein 2½
Vegetable ¾
10 Calories Optional Exchange

CHEESE AND YOGURT MOUSSE
Serves 2 (235 Calories per serving)

Almost any soft fruit can be used as a topping for this mousse. Kiwi fruit and strawberries or, alternatively, a combination of different coloured grapes, halved and seeded.

4oz (120g) curd cheese
2 tablespoons caster sugar
few drops of vanilla essence
1½ teaspoons gelatine
2 tablespoons hot water
¼ pint (150ml) low-fat natural yogurt
2 egg whites
pinch of salt
1 kiwi fruit, sliced
5oz (150g) strawberries, halved

① Beat the curd cheese, sugar and vanilla essence together.

② Sprinkle the gelatine over the hot water, stir. Stand the container in a saucepan of simmering water until the gelatine has dissolved.

③ Gradually beat the yogurt into the curd cheese mixture.

④ Stir a little of the curd cheese and yogurt into the dissolved gelatine, pour into the curd cheese mixture and mix well.

⑤ Whisk the egg whites with the salt until peaking. Fold into the cheese mixture using a metal spoon.

⑥ Divide between two wide dessert dishes and leave until set.

⑦ Decorate with the kiwi fruit and strawberries.

Exchanges per serving:
Fruit 1
Milk ½
Protein 1
80 Calories Optional Exchange

CHEESY CAULIFLOWER SOUP
Serves 2 (175 Calories per serving)

This filling soup gives two people very generous servings. It can easily be transported in an insulated flask to provide a warming lunchtime meal.

I small onion, chopped
½ medium cauliflower (about 10oz/300g), broken into florets
½ pint (300ml) vegetable stock
½ teaspoon chervil or 2 teaspoons freshly chopped chervil or salad burnet
good pinch freshly grated nutmeg
¼ pint (150ml) skimmed milk
2oz (60g) mature Cheddar cheese, grated
salt and pepper
few green or purple broccoli florets

① Place the onion, cauliflower, stock and chervil in a saucepan. Bring to the boil, reduce the heat, cover and simmer for 25 minutes.

② Pour the cauliflower, stock etc. into a blender or food processor and process until smooth. Transfer to a clean saucepan.

③ Stir in the nutmeg and milk. Bring to the boil, stirring all the time. Sprinkle in the cheese and season to taste. Stir until the cheese has melted.

④ Plunge the broccoli florets in boiling water for 2 minutes.

⑤ Serve the soup in warm bowls garnished with the broccoli florets.

Exchanges per serving:
Milk ¼
Protein 1
Vegetable 2

SULTANA CHEESE PUDDING
Serves 2 (230 Calories per serving)

Don't be surprised when the puddings rise during baking and then, as they cool, sink down and away from the sides of the ramekin. The pudding isn't meant to have the lightness of a soufflé. It is a delicious version of a cheesecake without the added calories of a pastry or biscuit base.

½ teaspoon margarine
4oz (120g) curd cheese
1 tablespoon caster sugar
grated zest of ½ a lemon
2 teaspoons lemon juice
1oz (30g) sultanas
1 egg, separated
pinch of salt
To serve
2 tablespoons soured cream
2 slices of lemon

① Grease two ¼-pint (150-ml) ramekins with the margarine.

② Beat together the curd cheese, sugar, lemon zest and juice, the sultanas and egg yolk.

③ In a separate bowl, whisk the egg white and salt until peaking.

④ Using a metal spoon, fold a tablespoon of egg white into the mixture, then fold in the remaining egg white.

⑤ Spoon the mixture into the 2 greased ramekins and bake at Gas Mark 3, 160°C, 325°F for 25–30 minutes until set and beginning to brown. Leave to cool in the ramekins, then turn out onto the serving plates and leave until completely cold.

⑥ Just before serving, top each cheese pudding with a tablespoon of soured cream and a twist of lemon.

Exchanges per serving:
Fat ¼
Fruit ½
Protein 1½
65 Calories Optional Exchange

SAVOURY BREAD PUDDING
Serves 2 (395 Calories per serving)

This savoury pudding is puffed up and golden brown when removed from the oven, so serve it immediately with a salad. Don't try to keep it warm – it will only sink and its appearance be spoilt.

2½ teaspoons margarine
3 × 1-oz (30-g) slices white or wholemeal bread
2oz (60g) thinly sliced cooked ham, cut into 1-inch (2.5-cm) squares
1oz (30g) cheese, grated
½ pint (300ml) skimmed milk
2 eggs, beaten
dash of chilli sauce
salt

① Use ½ teaspoon margarine to grease an ovenproof dish.

② Spread the bread thinly with the margarine, cut into strips.

③ Place layers of bread, ham and cheese in the dish, beginning and ending with bread. Reserve a little of the cheese.

④ Heat the milk until steaming, pour into the eggs, beating all the time. Season with chilli sauce and salt and strain over the bread pudding. Sprinkle over the reserved cheese. Leave to stand 20 minutes.

⑤ Bake at Gas Mark 4, 180°C, 350°F for about 30 minutes or until set and lightly golden brown. Serve at once.

Exchanges per serving:
Bread 1½
Fat 1¼
Milk ½
Protein 2½

PANCAKES
Serves 2 (210 Calories per serving)

Pancakes take a lot of practice to make well. They should be very thin, not thick and stodgy. They may be eaten on their own with a squeeze of lemon and sprinkling of sugar or used as the basis for a dessert such as Brandied Apricots Flambé (page 182) or stuffed with a savoury filling such as Savoury Minced Beef (page 53).

2oz (60g) plain flour
pinch of salt
1 egg, beaten
¼ pint (150ml) skimmed milk
2 teaspoons margarine or vegetable oil

① Sieve the flour and salt into a bowl, make a well in the centre, add the egg, and gradually beat or whisk in the milk. Put to one side.

② Prove a 7-inch (18-cm) frying pan. This will help to prevent the pancakes sticking and reduce the amount of oil required for cooking them. Generously sprinkle salt over the base of the frying pan, heat gently, tip out the salt, then wipe thoroughly with a pad of kitchen paper. Heat a small amount of margarine or oil in the pan and once again wipe round the pan.

③ Heat a little margarine in the pan, pour in the batter whilst turning the pan so it thinly coats the base. Cook over a moderate heat until the underside is golden, toss or turn over and cook the other side.

④ Transfer the cooked pancake to a plate, cover and keep warm in a low oven while repeating the procedure. This quantity should make 7 or 8 pancakes.

Exchanges per serving:
Bread 1
Fat 1
Milk ¼
Protein ½

SWEET CHEESE PANCAKES
Serves 2 (195 Calories per serving)

I have suggested that these little pancakes are served with maple syrup or honey, but if you prefer they could be sprinkled with the same quantity of caster sugar. This would provide the same Exchanges quoted below.

2oz (60g) curd or low-fat soft cheese
1 egg, separated
1 tablespoon plain flour
2 teaspoons caster sugar
½ teaspoon finely grated lemon zest
2 teaspoons lemon juice
good pinch cinnamon
pinch of salt
2 teaspoons vegetable oil
2 teaspoons clear honey or maple syrup

① Cream the curd cheese and egg yolk together in a bowl.

② Mix in the flour, sugar, lemon zest and juice and cinnamon.

③ Whisk the egg white and salt until peaking. Fold a little into the cheese mixture, using a metal spoon – this will lighten the mixture – then fold in the remaining egg white.

④ Heat 1 teaspoon of oil in a small frying pan, drop 2 tablespoons of the mixture into the hot oil and cook over a moderate heat until the underside is golden brown. Turn over and cook the other side.

⑤ Transfer the cooked pancakes to a warm plate. Heat the remaining oil and repeat the process with the rest of the mixture.

⑥ Serve the pancakes with the honey or maple syrup trickled over the top.

> *Exchanges per serving:*
> Fat 1
> Protein 1
> 55 Calories Optional Exchange

BAKED EGG CUSTARD
Serves 2 (130 Calories per serving)

I always bake egg custards standing in a pan of hot water to ensure the eggs won't reach too high a temperature and curdle. This plain custard is the perfect accompaniment to stewed fruit.

¼ teaspoon margarine
1 egg, beaten
1 tablespoon caster sugar
½ pint (300ml) skimmed milk
freshly grated nutmeg

① Grease a ¾-pint (450-ml) pie dish or ovenproof dish with the margarine.

② Beat together the egg, sugar and a tablespoon of milk.

③ Heat the remaining milk until steaming, stir into the egg mixture.

④ Strain the custard into the greased dish and sprinkle with the freshly grated nutmeg.

⑤ Stand the dish in a baking tin containing warm to hot water to a depth of ½ inch (1.25 cm). Bake at Gas Mark 3, 160°C, 325°F for about 40 minutes. To check the custard is set, make a slit in the top with a knife and gently press each side of the slit. If no milk oozes out, the custard is cooked.

Exchanges per serving:
Milk ½
Protein ½
40 Calories Optional Exchange

MERINGUE BASKETS
Serves 3 (85 Calories per serving)

These meringue baskets can be filled with a variety of fresh fruits. Blueberries or a mixture of strawberries and kiwi fruit look particularly attractive.

I egg white
pinch of salt
4 tablespoons caster sugar

① Line a baking sheet with non-stick baking parchment.

② Whisk the egg white and salt in a bowl until peaking, add a tablespoon of caster sugar and continue whisking until the egg white forms peaks again.

③ Sprinkle in another tablespoon of caster sugar and whisk again until the same consistency is obtained. Fold in the remaining sugar with a metal spoon.

④ Transfer the meringue mixture to a piping bag fitted with a ½-inch (1.25-cm) fluted nozzle. Pipe a circle about 3 inches (7.5 cm) in diameter, pipe one or two rings on top of each other around the edge of the base circle to form a basket. There will be sufficient meringue to make three baskets.

⑤ Bake at Gas Mark ¼, 130°C, 250°F for about 3 hours until the meringues are firm and crisp but still white. If they begin to colour, open the oven door a little.

⑥ Cool on a wire rack and either store in an airtight tin or fill with fruit and serve.

Exchanges per serving:
90 Calories Optional Exchange

STRAWBERRY SOUFFLÉ OMELETTE
Serves 1 (280 Calories per serving)

The filling for this omelette is sliced strawberries and honey, but other fruits may be used, or spread a tablespoon of jam over half the omelette before folding. If you decide to alter the recipe, remember to alter the Exchanges.

2 eggs, separated
1 teaspoon caster sugar
1 teaspoon margarine
pinch of salt
2½oz (75g) strawberries, sliced
1 teaspoon clear honey

① Beat the egg yolks and caster sugar together.

② Melt the margarine over a low heat in a 7½–8-inch (19–20-cm) omelette pan.

③ While the margarine is melting, whisk the egg whites and salt until peaking, fold them into the yolks.

④ Pour the egg mixture into the pan and cook over a low heat until the underside is golden brown.

⑤ Transfer the pan to a preheated grill and cook until the omelette is browned on top. Remove at once and mark across the centre with a spatula or knife.

⑥ Arrange the strawberries over half the omelette, trickle the honey over the fruit and fold the omelette over. Serve immediately.

Exchanges per serving:
Fat 1
Fruit ½
Protein 2
40 Calories Optional Exchange

MEAT AND POULTRY

The term meat includes the flesh and internal organs of all animals, poultry and game. It is an excellent source of protein and therefore an important food to include in one's diet.

Choose meat carefully. Look for an even colour and never buy meat which smells unpleasantly or is standing in its own juices. Unwrap the meat, transfer it to a plate, cover loosely and store in the cool, if possible in the refrigerator. Never keep meat in a warm room as it will deteriorate very quickly. Use minced meat, sausages, offal and poultry as soon as possible, preferably within a day of purchase. Other meats should be cooked within 2–3 days.

Once meat has been cooked, if it is to be stored, cool it quickly, cover and place in the refrigerator. Stews, casseroles, etc., must be brought to the boil and thoroughly reheated. They should be simmered for at least ten minutes.

All the weights for meat given in recipes are for meat purchased raw and trimmed of all fat.

BEEF

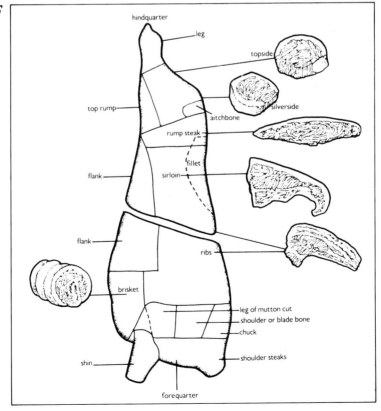

Beef, Veal, Lamb, Pork

What to look for

Take note of the colour of the meat, which is an indication of freshness. Beef should be deep red, veal a pinky beige, lamb between pink and red, pork pale pink and bacon a pinky brown with no discoloured patches.

The amount of fat varies according to the meat and its cut; for example, pork contains a lot more fat than veal. It is for this reason that meat must be grilled, baked or roasted on a rack, or boiled and then cooled. This ensures the fat either runs out of the meat and drips through a rack or solidifies when the cooking liquid is cooled and can be lifted off. When using minced meat, form it into small patties and grill, turning once, until the fat stops dripping from each patty.

Beef: Choose beef which is a deep red colour with small flecks of fat dispersed in the lean meat. Avoid cuts which contain gristle; this is a sign that the meat was from an old animal and will be tough. The following chart explains which cuts are most suitable for particular cooking methods.

BEEF

Cut	Description	Suitable Methods of Cooking
Rump	A steak cut from the hindquarter beside the sirloin.	Full of flavour but not as tender as fillet, so advisable to marinate before cooking. Suitable for grilling.
Sirloin joint	A large joint taken from the ribs. Sold on or off the bone.	Very tender, ideal for roasting.
Sirloin steaks	Porterhouse – taken from the thick end of the sirloin. When cooked on the bone it is called a T-bone steak.	Tender, ideal for grilling.
	Minute – a very thin steak from the thin end of the sirloin.	Tender, ideal for grilling.
Fillet	The undercut of the sirloin. The Chateaubriand is a thick slice taken from the middle of the fillet.	Tender, ideal for grilling.
Ribs	A large joint taken from next to the sirloin. Sold on or off the bone.	Not as tender as sirloin but has a good flavour. Pot-roast, roast, braise or boil.
Entrecôte	A cut of meat taken from between the ribs, but sirloin and rump steaks sometimes sold under this name.	Tender, ideal for grilling.
Topside	A lean joint taken from the hindquarter. Usually sold boned and rolled.	Not so tender as sirloin. Most suited to braising or pot-roasting.
Silverside	A boneless joint from the	Requires long slow cooking either

	hindquarter, beside the topside. Also sold salted.	by boiling or braising. Salted silverside is the traditional cut for boiled beef and carrots.
Aitchbone	A large, rather fatty joint from the hindquarter with a large bone, but sometimes sold boned and rolled. Also sold salted.	Usually roasted but may be boiled or braised. A salted aitchbone is boiled.
Brisket	A rather fatty joint from the forequarter, sold on or off the bone. Often sold salted.	Has a good flavour but requires slow roasting or braising. Salted brisket is boiled.
Flank	Thick and thin flank is cut from the belly.	Tends to be coarse and requires slow moist cooking. Ideal for stews, pot-roasting and braising.
Leg and Shin	The meat is usually lean but contains a lot of bone.	Tends to be fairly coarse, therefore requires slow moist cooking. Ideal for stews.
Chuck or Blade Steak	A boneless, fairly lean cut taken from the shoulder.	Suitable for casseroles and stews. Requires moist method of cooking.

Veal: Choose veal which is a pinky beige in colour with a fine, soft, moist texture. It should not be mottled. There should be very little fat as veal comes from very young animals.

VEAL

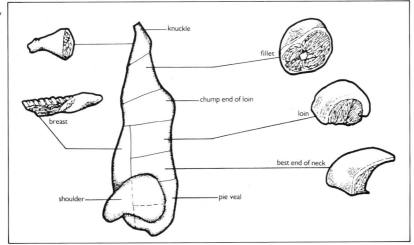

Cut	Description	Suitable Methods of Cooking
Leg	Sold on or off the bone.	A prime cut often stuffed before roasting.

Fillet Joint	Sold on or off the bone for roasting as a joint.	A prime cut usually stuffed before roasting.
Fillet Slices	Cut in slices, also called escalopes.	Often beaten very thin and fried, or cut in strips and incorporated in stir-frys. May be grilled.
Loin	Sold on or off the bone.	Roasted on the bone or, if off the bone, stuffed before roasting.
Cutlets	Good quality cuts taken from the top of the loin near the neck.	Suitable for grilling or braising.
Chops	Loin chops differ in shape according to which part of the loin they are taken from.	Suitable for grilling.
Shoulder	An awkward shaped joint which requires boning and stuffing.	Suitable for roasting.
Best End of Neck	Sold on or off the bone.	Roast or braise on the bone, or boned and stuffed. Alternatively bone, cut into pieces and stew or braise.
Knuckle	Sold on the bone, a cut from the foreleg.	Boil, stew or bone, stuff and braise.
Breast	Sold on or off the bone.	Usually boned, stuffed and roasted.
Scrag and Pie Veal	Trimmings from various parts of the animal removed when preparing joints, chops etc.	Suitable for stewing and adding to pies as its name implies.

Lamb: Choose lamb which is a pinky red colour. The lighter the colour, the younger the animal.

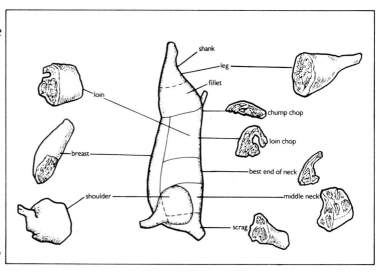

LAMB

Cut	Description	Suitable Methods of Cooking
Leg	Sold on or off the bone. Also available cut into leg steaks.	Suitable for roasting, stewing, casseroling etc. May be cut in chunks and used to make kebabs. Leg steaks are usually grilled.
Loin	Sold on or off the bone.	Full of flavour, usually roasted on the bone or boned, stuffed and roasted.
Chops	Cut from the loin, the chops nearest the leg are chump chops.	Good flavour. Suitable for grilling, stewing or casseroling.
Best End of Neck	Sold as a whole joint or cut into cutlets, the joint next to the loin.	The joint is usually roasted or braised. Two pieces of best end of neck are chopped and sliced between the bones to make the traditional 'crown roast of lamb', or chined and formed into an arch to form a 'guard of honour'. Individual cutlets are usually grilled.
Shoulder	A large joint with quite a lot of fat.	Usually roasted but may be boned and cut into cubes for making kebabs and using in casseroles etc.
Breast	A fatty joint with a lot of bone.	Usually boned, stuffed and rolled, then slow roasted, braised, stewed or boiled.
Middle and Scrag End	These cuts are rather fatty and contain a high proportion of bone.	Ideal for stews and casseroles as the meat has a good flavour.

Pork: Choose pork which is pale pink with a slight marbling of fat. The bones should also have a slight pink tinge; this indicates it is the meat of a young animal.

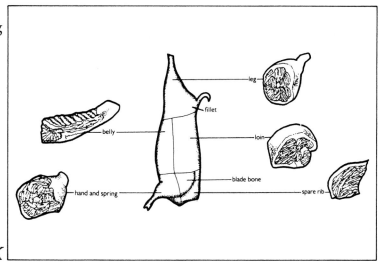

PORK

Cut	Description	Suitable Methods of Cooking
Leg	A very large joint, frequently cut into two smaller joints. Sold on or off the bone.	Ideal for roasting as a whole joint or boned and stuffed.
Fillet	Taken from the top of the hind leg, it has a central bone. Tenderloin or pork fillet is sold in a piece or in thin slices.	May be left on the bone and roasted or boned, stuffed and roasted. The piece of tenderloin may be roasted and the slices are best grilled or incorporated in stir-fries or casseroles.
Loin Joint	Sold on or off the bone. Often has the kidney attached.	Ideal for roasting on the bone or may be boned, stuffed and roasted.
Loin Chops	Also sold as chops which may have a kidney attached.	Usually grilled or casseroled.
Spare Rib Joint	Sold on the bone as a joint but may be boned and sold in pieces.	Roast the whole joint but use the cut meat in braising, casseroles or stews.
Spare Rib Cutlets	The spare rib may be cut into cutlets which have very little or no bone.	Grill or use in casseroles.
Hand and Spring	This makes up the foreleg, sold on the bone.	May be roasted, boiled or stewed.
Blade	The cut taken above the hand and spring. Sold on the bone.	Suitable for roasting.
Belly	A fat cut sometimes sold salted.	May be roasted but usually boiled and eaten cold.
Spare Ribs	A cut taken from the belly which has a large proportion of bone to meat. The meat is between the rib bones.	Usually barbecued.

Bacon: Bacon is cured fresh pork. The animals are specially bred to have large gammons, long backs and small shoulders with smaller bones than other pigs. The curing can be carried out in a variety of ways but it is usually a combination of injecting brine and dry salting, then immersion in brine followed by maturation when the pork develops a pale rind with the pinky brown bacon colour. This process may be followed by smoking which gives the meat a firmer texture, smoked flavour and brown rind.

There is frequently confusion between bacon and ham. Bacon is the cured pig, ham is strictly speaking the leg of the pig which is cured and matured on its own without the rest of the carcass. Smoked hams may be sold cooked or uncooked. Hams such as York or Wiltshire, if purchased fresh, require soaking for 12–24 hours, depending on the type of curing, before cooking.

Good bacon has a pleasing aroma and the areas of fat should always be white and firm. Unsmoked bacon is often called 'green'. The cuts of bacon vary from one part of the country to another but the following can be used as a guide:

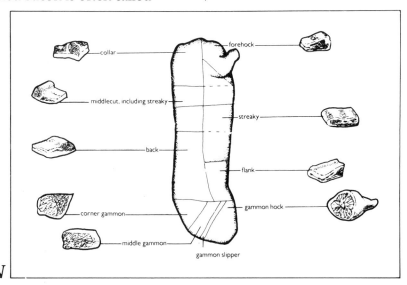

BACON

Cut	Description	Suitable Methods of Cooking
Streaky	Narrow rashers of fat and lean meat. Sometimes sold in a piece.	May be boiled in the piece or grilled as rashers. Not suitable for Weight Watchers recipes.
Middlecut	Long rashers joining the back and streaky cuts. Sold in the piece as a joint.	Stuff the joint and boil or roast.
Back	A lean piece of meat with a separate layer of fat above. Available as a piece or rashers.	The piece of back is suitable for boiling. Rashers may be grilled.
Bacon Chops	Boneless rib chops about ½ inch (1.25cm) thick.	Ideal for grilling.
Collar Joints	The collar is a very large joint which is usually sold in two pieces, the end of collar and prime collar.	Usually boiled, roasted or braised.
Collar Rashers	Thin slices of collar are sold as rashers. They have more lean than fat.	Ideal for grilling.
Forehock	Sold on or off the bone. The knuckle may be removed and sold separately.	The joints are ideal for boiling or roasting. The knuckle is suitable for stocks and soups.

Gammon Joints	The gammon is a very big joint which can be divided into corner, middle and slipper gammons and a gammon hock. The gammon knuckle is meatier than the forehock knuckle.	The gammon is lean with a good flavour and fine texture. It may be braised, boiled and roasted or cut into pieces and added to casseroles and stews.
Gammon Rashers	Very lean thin cuts.	Ideal for grilling.

Offal

The term 'offal' is used to describe the internal organs of animals. The most commonly used offal are the following:

Liver: Ox, calf's, lamb's, pig's and chicken liver are used in casseroles and stews. Chicken, lamb's and calf's livers have a more delicate flavour, and are suitable for grilling and making into patés. Cut out any blood vessels with scissors.

Kidney: Ox, calf's, lamb's and pig's kidneys are used in casseroles and stews. Remove the outer skin, cut almost in half from the rounded side towards the core, remove the core with scissors.

Heart: Ox and calf's hearts need slow cooking. The ox heart may be purchased in slices and added to stews, the calf's heart may be slowly roasted, braised or stewed. Lamb's hearts are more tender and may be stuffed, braised or roasted. Cut away the large blood vessels and soak in salted water for 5–10 minutes to remove the blood. Rinse before use.

Tongue: Ox tongue is often sold salted and boiled, sheep's tongues are stewed or boiled. Tongues are usually salted before being sold and therefore should be soaked 1–2 hours before use. Remove excess fat before cooking. After cooking, trim away the fat and windpipes and any tiny bones.

Tripe: Tripe is the lining of the ox's stomach. It is usually sold 'dressed' which means cleaned and par-boiled. It lacks flavour and requires stewing with ingredients which are full of flavour such as onions.

Sweetbreads: There are two kinds of sweetbreads, the pancreas and the thymus gland. Blanch the sweetbreads by plunging in boiling water, drain and place in cold water. This hardens the fat which can then be removed. Sweetbreads are usually stewed.

Brains: Calf's brains may be poached and served with a sauce. Lamb's brains are more often stewed.

Oxtail: This has a high proportion of bone and tends to be fatty but makes an excellent soup or stew. Choose a tail with bright red meat and creamy white fat.

Poultry

Poultry includes chicken, turkey, guinea fowl, ducks and geese, sold whole or jointed. Poultry may be cooked with its skin on, but it is advisable to remove it before eating as a great deal of fat is stored under the skin.

There are many different types of chicken: poussins are very small young chickens suitable for 1 or 2 people; broilers are small birds suitable for serving 3 to 4 people; boiling chickens are eighteen months or more old, and are therefore only suitable for casseroles; large fattened chickens are available and suitable for feeding 6 to 10 people; large roasters are usually young cockerels or hens, suitable for feeding 5 to 6 people. Chickens and turkeys are also sold as joints, in quarters or boneless fillets.

Turkeys, guinea fowl, ducks and geese are usually sold plucked and oven-ready. Guinea fowl are most suited to moist methods of cooking such as casseroling. They require a lot of fat and frequent basting to roast well.

What to look for when choosing fresh poultry

Check that the skin is evenly coloured, not patchy, with no unpleasant smell. The body and legs should be well rounded and plump, the end of the breast bone pliable and the feet soft and smooth, unless the bird is old, for example a boiling chicken.

Game

Game is the term given to animals and birds protected by the law. There are certain seasons when it is legal to hunt and kill game. Rabbits and pigeons are not strictly included under this heading but rabbits are cooked in the same way as hares, and pigeons in the same way as wild or wood pigeons, so they are included with the other animals.

Game is available frozen most of the year but the seasons for hunting game vary, for example partridge may only be killed between September 1st and February 1st, but hare may only be hunted between August 1st and the end of February.

Game birds are usually roasted, braised or casseroled.

Venison may be roasted or stewed. The best joint for roasting is the saddle but the shoulder is better suited to stewing.

Rabbits and hares may be jointed then casseroled, braised, made into pies etc.

Only young animals are suitable for roasting.

Methods of cookery suitable for meat and poultry

Roasting or Baking: This is suitable for prime cuts of meat and poultry weighing over 1½lbs (720g) and coated with a layer of fat. Traditionally meat was always roasted on a spit but this is now carried out in an oven or on a rotisserie in an oven. There are different methods of roasting but always place the joint on a rack in the roasting tin with the thickest layer of fat on top: this will automatically baste the joint as it melts and runs down the meat. Meat placed in a preheated hot oven tends to shrink considerably and the meat becomes tough compared with meat placed in a cold oven and gradually heated to about Gas Mark 6, 220°C, 400°F. This cold oven method results in less shrinkage and fairly tender meat with a good flavour. When roasting chicken or turkey, lay it on one side of its breast for one third of the cooking time, on the other side of its breast for another third, and the remaining third on its back. This will help to keep the breast moist. Meat may be roasted in roasting bags, foil or a closed tin but it does not have the traditional roasted appearance as it has cooked in its own juices. If this method is used, always remove the covering for the last thirty minutes of cooking. Meat thermometers are useful to achieve the desired result, particularly if a rare joint is required. Insert the thermometer into the thickest part of the meat, but make sure it does not touch the bone. The following chart describes how different meats appear at particular temperatures:

Beef	60°C (140°F)	Very rare when hot, ideal for a moist cold joint.
	75°C (160°F)	Rare, brownish meat with bloody juices, retains a pink tinge when cold.

	77°C (170°F)	Well done, rather dry when cold.
	82°C (180°F)	Very well done, fat rendered down and fibres breaking up.
Veal	82°C (180°F)	Pale, moist meat.
Lamb	82°C (180°F)	Brown, moist meat.
Pork	89°C (190°F)	Pale, moist meat.

Pot-roasting is only possible in heavy-based saucepans and in a depth of ¼ inch (5mm) of fat. The meat should be browned on all sides, then cooked over a low heat and basted and turned occasionally. Suitable meats are compact joints with a layer of fat, for example, brisket and topside. The time is calculated as for oven roasting. For the slow oven method described above, weigh the meat when stuffed and allow 20 minutes for the oven to heat up with the meat in it, then allow the following:

Beef	– thick cuts, 20 minutes per lb (500g), plus 20 minutes over thin cuts, 25 minutes per lb (500g), plus 15 minutes over
Lamb	– thick cuts, 20 minutes per lb (500g), plus 20 minutes over thin cuts, 15 minutes per lb (500g), plus 15 minutes over
Pork	– all cuts, 30 minutes per lb (500g), plus 30 minutes over
Veal	– thick cuts, 30 minutes per lb (500g), plus 30 minutes over thin cuts, 25 minutes per lb (500g), plus 25 minutes over
Chicken	– 20 minutes per lb (500g), plus 20 minutes over

Braising: This method of cooking is suitable for prime and secondary cuts as it combines stewing, steaming and roasting. The meat, poultry or game is cooked in a saucepan or casserole on top of a bed of vegetables with sufficient liquid to keep the contents moist. Braising can take place on the hob or in an oven. To achieve a roasted appearance, remove the lid from the casserole and increase the heat to Gas Mark 7, 210°C, 425°F for the last 25–30 minutes of cooking.

Boiling: The meat is covered with cold water and sometimes vegetables are added. The water is slowly brought to boiling point, covered tightly and simmered for the recommended time.

Stewing: The meat is cut into small cubes or strips, mixed with vegetables and liquid is added. It is a long, slow method of cooking which requires a heavy saucepan or casserole to prevent burning and a tight-fitting lid to prevent the liquid evaporating. The temperature must be kept below boiling point but the stewing may take place on the hob or in the oven.

Grilling: This is a quick method of cooking, suitable for tender meat. Season with salt and pepper and place under a preheated grill. It may be necessary to brush some meats with a little oil to prevent them becoming dry and tough.

Frying: This is not suitable for Weight Watchers recipes, apart from the stir-frying of strips of meat for a very short time in a measured amount of oil or margarine.

1 Chicken legs
2 Lamb, leg steaks
3 Pork, loin chops
4 Beef, flank
5 Minced pork

BEEF STROGANOFF
Serves 2 (300 Calories per serving)

Take care not to overcook the beef. After its initial grilling to remove the fat, it needs only a little extra cooking.

2 teaspoons vegetable oil
I small onion, thinly sliced
3oz (90g) button mushrooms, sliced
7oz (210g) rump steak, thinly sliced
4½ tablespoons soured cream
pepper

① Heat the oil. Add the onion and sauté for 2–3 minutes until soft.

② Add the mushrooms and steak and continue stirring over a moderate heat for about 4 minutes until the mushrooms and steak are cooked through.

③ Remove from the heat, stir in the soured cream and season with pepper.

> *Exchanges per serving:*
> Fat I
> Protein 2½
> Vegetable I
> 75 Calories Optional Exchange

SAVOURY MINCED BEEF
Serves 2 (270 Calories per serving)

This is a very simple, basic recipe. Add a chopped garlic clove and a bouquet garni for extra flavour or add 1–2 tablespoons of tomato purée, but remember to add an extra 5–10 Calories Optional Exchange per serving. This recipe is very useful as a stuffing for pancakes.

8oz (240g) minced beef
3oz (90g) onion, chopped
3oz (90g) carrot, diced
3oz (90g) shelled peas
I stick celery, sliced
I ½oz (45g) mushrooms, sliced
I tablespoon flour
¼ pint (150ml) beef stock
¼ teaspoon mixed dried herbs
salt and pepper

① Crumble the beef patties into a saucepan.

② Mix in the prepared vegetables.

③ Sprinkle in the flour and stir well. Gradually add the stock. Season with the herbs, salt and pepper.

④ Bring to the boil, stirring all the time. Cover, reduce the heat and simmer for 20 minutes, stirring occasionally.

> *Exchanges per serving:*
> Protein 3
> Vegetable 2
> 15 Calories Optional Exchange

BEEF STEW
Serves 2 (300 Calories per serving)

This is a basic recipe which is made on the top of the stove.

8oz (240g) braising steak
2 teaspoons vegetable oil
1 onion, sliced
½oz (15g) flour
3oz (90g) carrot, thickly sliced
9oz (270g) mixture of turnip and swede, cubed
½ teaspoon mixed herbs
½ pint (300ml) vegetable or beef stock
salt and pepper

① Cut the grilled or baked braising steak into 1-inch (2.5-cm) cubes.

② Heat the oil in a saucepan, add the onion and stir-fry 2–3 minutes.

③ Stir in the flour and mix well. Add the vegetables, herbs and beef and gradually stir in the stock. Season well with salt and pepper.

④ Bring to the boil, reduce the heat, cover and simmer very gently for 45 minutes.

Exchanges per serving:
Fat 1
Bread ¼
Protein 3
Vegetable 2½

CORNED BEEF CUPS
Serves 2 (210 Calories per serving)

If you are using the oven at any temperature between Gas Mark 4–6, 180°–200°C, 350°–400°F, this is a simple snack to make. Just wash the potato, prick through the skin and bake for about an hour. If you own a microwave it is possible to cook the potato in a few minutes.

6-oz (180-g) hot baked potato
3oz (90g) corned beef
1 tablespoon chopped spring onion
1 egg, beaten
salt and pepper

① Cut the potato in half lengthways. Carefully scoop out the potato leaving the skin intact.

② Mash the corned beef in a bowl. Add the potato and spring onion and mash once again.

③ Gradually add the beaten egg. Season the filling well.

④ Spoon the stuffing back into the potato skins and reheat under a moderate grill for 5–6 minutes until the stuffing is piping hot and browning on top. Serve with a crisp green or mixed salad.

> Exchanges per serving:
> Bread 1
> Protein 2

VEAL ESCALOPES WITH LEEK AND MUSHROOM SAUCE

Serves 2 (210 Calories per serving)

This recipe is easy to make and ideal for a special occasion. Serve with freshly cooked vegetables such as mangetout or green beans and carrots.

2 × 4-oz (120-g) veal escalopes
1 teaspoon lemon juice
For the sauce
1 teaspoon margarine
1 small leek, thinly sliced
3oz (90g) button mushrooms, sliced
3 tablespoons single cream
2 teaspoons chopped parsley
squeeze of lemon juice
salt and pepper
lemon wedges to serve

① Place the veal escalopes on a grill rack, sprinkle over half the lemon juice and grill under a moderate heat for about 4 minutes. Turn over, sprinkle over the remaining lemon juice and grill for a further 4–5 minutes.

② Meanwhile, make the sauce. Heat the margarine, add the leek and stir-fry for 3 minutes. Add the mushrooms and continue stir-frying for 2–3 minutes.

③ Stir the cream and parsley into the sauce. Season to taste with the lemon juice, salt and pepper. Reheat, stirring all the time.

④ Serve the veal escalopes on warm serving plates with the sauce poured over and garnished with lemon wedges.

Exchanges per serving:

Fat ½

Protein 3

Vegetable 1

50 Calories Optional Exchange

SHEPHERD'S PIE
Serves 2 (365 Calories per serving)

Some people claim a shepherd wouldn't use lamb for this dish, others that he wouldn't consider any other meat but lamb. Some say the meat should be minced, others sliced; some state the meat should be cooked, others disagree. I've used minced lamb and precooked it in the normal way.

I teaspoon oil
I small onion, chopped
3oz (90g) carrot, diced
2 teaspoons flour
8oz (240g) minced lamb, crumbled
½ teaspoon basil
½ teaspoon marjoram
I small can tomatoes
salt and pepper
9oz (270g) peeled potatoes
I tablespoon skimmed milk

① Heat the oil in a saucepan, add the onion and stir-fry for 3–4 minutes. Add the carrots and stir over a moderate heat for a further 2 minutes.

② Sprinkle in the flour, add the lamb and herbs and stir in the canned tomatoes, breaking up the tomatoes with a spoon. Season well and bring to the boil.

③ Meanwhile, boil the potatoes in salted water until cooked, drain and mash with the skimmed milk, season with salt and pepper.

④ Place the mince mixture in an ovenproof dish, cover with the mashed potatoes and roughen the surface with a fork. Bake at Gas Mark 5, 190°C, 375°F, for 25 minutes. Place under a preheated grill to brown.

> *Exchanges per serving:*
> Bread 1½
> Fat ½
> Protein 3½
> Vegetable 2½
> 15 Calories Optional Exchange

Shepherd's Pie

SWEET AND SOUR PORK
Serves 2 (255 Calories per serving)

Serve this dish with boiled rice to make a complete meal. It looks most attractive garnished with spring onion curls which are made by making small cuts through the light green leaves to the bulbous end, removing the roots and placing in cold water for 15–20 minutes.

For the pork balls
9oz (270g) minced pork
I clove garlic, crushed
good pinch of rosemary
salt and pepper
For the sauce
I tablespoon cornflour
2 tablespoons soy sauce
2 tablespoons wine or cider vinegar
I tablespoon tomato purée
I tablespoon chopped spring onion
½ green or red pepper, or a mixture of both, cored and finely chopped
4oz (120g) fresh pineapple, cored and chopped
¼ pint (150ml) vegetable stock
spring onion curls to garnish

① Mix the pork and seasonings together, shape into eight balls, grill until the fat stops dripping, turning from time to time.

② Blend the cornflour with the soy sauce, vinegar and tomato purée. Stir in the spring onion, peppers, pineapple and stock.

③ Bring to the boil, stirring all the time, reduce the heat, cover and simmer for 5–6 minutes.

④ Add the pork balls, cover and simmer for a further 5–10 minutes. Serve garnished with spring onion curls.

> *Exchanges per serving:*
> Fruit ½
> Protein 3½
> Vegetable ½
> 20 Calories Optional Exchange

LAMB-FILLED AUBERGINE
Serves 2 (260 Calories per serving)

For a change, sprinkle ½oz (15g) grated cheese on top of each aubergine half about 5 minutes before the end of the cooking time. Break the patties of mince up well to ensure the meat is evenly distributed throughout the filling.

9-oz (270-g) aubergine
salt
2 teaspoons vegetable oil
I clove garlic, finely chopped
I small onion or shallot, chopped
½oz (15g) fresh breadcrumbs
7oz (210g) minced lamb
I ½ tablespoons chopped mint
I tablespoon tomato purée
salt and pepper
¼ pint (150ml) vegetable or chicken stock

① Cut the aubergine in half lengthways. Score into the white flesh and sprinkle liberally with salt, leave 20–30 minutes then rinse well.

② Remove the white flesh from the aubergine leaving the skin intact. A grapefruit knife is useful for this job. Chop the flesh.

③ Heat the oil, add the garlic and onion and stir over a moderate heat for 2–3 minutes. Add the chopped aubergine and stir round for a further 2 minutes.

④ Mix in the breadcrumbs, lamb, mint and tomato purée. Season well.

⑤ Spoon the filling back into the aubergine skins and transfer to an ovenproof dish which holds them snugly. Pour the stock round the aubergines and cover with foil. Bake at Gas Mark 5, 190°C, 375°F for 20–25 minutes.

Exchanges per serving:
Bread ¼
Fat I
Protein 2½
Vegetable 2
5 Calories Optional Exchange

LAMB WITH FRUIT SAUCE
Serves 2 (225 Calories per serving)

The combination of cranberries, orange juice and redcurrant jelly complements the flavour of lamb. Don't be tempted to add more sugar to the sauce; there is sufficient in the redcurrant jelly to sweeten but still leave a slight tart flavour.

2 × 4-oz (120-g) lamb steaks or chump chops
For the sauce
3 tablespoons fresh orange juice
3oz (90g) cranberries
2 tablespoons redcurrant jelly
½ teaspoon arrowroot
1 teaspoon water

① Grill the lamb while making the sauce.

② Place the orange juice and cranberries into a small saucepan, simmer gently for about 5 minutes until the cranberries start popping. Add the redcurrant jelly and stir round until dissolved.

③ Blend the arrowroot to a paste with the water, stir into the cranberries and bring to the boil, stirring all the time. Boil for 1 minute.

④ Serve the lamb chops on warm serving plates with the fruit sauce.

Exchanges per serving:

Fruit ½

Protein 3

55 Calories Optional Exchange

PORK AND PINEAPPLE STEW
Serves 2 (310 Calories per serving)

If fresh pineapple is very expensive or unavailable, substitute the unsweetened canned pineapple. It will still give a pleasant tang to the stew.

2 teaspoons vegetable oil
I clove garlic, finely chopped
I small onion, sliced
I small red pepper, cored and sliced
I stick celery, chopped
2 teaspoons flour
9oz (270g) pork tenderloin, cubed
I small can tomatoes
4oz (120g) fresh pineapple, cubed
4fl oz (120ml) vegetable or chicken stock
chopped celery leaves to garnish

① Heat the oil in a saucepan. Add the garlic and onion and stir for 2 minutes.

② Add all the remaining ingredients and bring to the boil, stirring all the time. Reduce the heat, cover and simmer 35–40 minutes.

③ Serve sprinkled with the chopped celery leaves.

Exchanges per serving:
Fat I
Fruit ½
Protein 3½
Vegetable 2½
10 Calories Optional Exchange

HAM STEAK WITH ORANGE AND APRICOT SAUCE
Serves 2 (200 Calories per serving)

The combination of oranges and apricots complements the flavour of the ham steaks. The sauce can also be used to accompany either boiled or roasted gammon.

4fl oz (120ml) orange and apricot juice
2oz (60g) dried apricots, chopped
1 teaspoon cornflour
4 tablespoons water
lemon juice to taste
2 × 4-oz (120-g) ham steaks

① Pour the orange and apricot juice into a bowl, add the chopped apricots and leave to soak for about 4 hours or overnight.

② Blend the cornflour to a paste with the water. Stir into the orange and apricot juice. Bring to the boil, stirring all the time, reduce the heat and simmer for 2 minutes. Add lemon juice to taste.

③ While the sauce is being made, grill the ham steaks for about 8 minutes, turning once.

④ Serve the ham steaks on warm serving plates with the sauce poured over. Garnish with slices of orange and sprigs of watercress.

Exchanges per serving:
Fruit 1½
Protein 3
5 Calories Optional Exchange

LIVER STIR-UP
Serves 2 (305 Calories per serving)

This family favourite can be adapted to use up any vegetables from the garden or vegetable basket. It can also be made from pig's or lamb's kidneys.

½oz (15g) flour
salt and pepper
6oz (180g) lamb's liver, thinly sliced
2 teaspoons vegetable oil
I small onion, thinly sliced
I × I-oz (30-g) rasher lean back bacon, grilled and cut into strips
I small carrot, cut into thin strips
I small courgette, sliced
4 tablespoons vegetable, lamb or chicken stock
5 tablespoons low-fat natural yogurt

① Season the flour with salt and pepper. Turn the liver in the seasoned flour, put to one side.

② Heat the oil in a saucepan, add the onion and sauté 2–3 minutes.

③ Add the liver and stir-fry for 2 minutes until brown.

④ Stir in the bacon, vegetables and stock. Bring to the boil, reduce the heat, cover and simmer for 5 minutes.

⑤ Remove from the heat, stir in the yogurt and serve.

Exchanges per serving:
Fat 1
Bread ¼
Protein 2½
Vegetable 1½
25 Calories Optional Exchange

DEVILLED KIDNEYS
Serves 2 (270 Calories per serving)

These kidneys are delicious served with boiled rice. Boil 1½oz (45g) long grain rice and serve with the dish. This would increase the Bread Exchange to 1 per serving.

12oz (360g) lamb's kidneys
½oz (15g) flour
salt and pepper
pinch of oregano
1 tablespoon oil
1 small onion, chopped
1 green pepper, cored and cut in strips
¼ pint (150ml) vegetable, lamb or chicken stock
1 teaspoon English mustard
2 teaspoons Worcestershire sauce

① Remove the skin from the kidneys, cut in half lengthways and cut out the white cores.

② Season the flour with salt, pepper and oregano, turn the kidney halves in the seasoned flour.

③ Heat the oil in a saucepan, add the onion and stir-fry for 1–2 minutes.

④ Add the kidneys and pepper and continue stirring over a moderate heat until the kidneys are lightly browned.

⑤ Stir in any remaining flour, the stock, mustard and Worcestershire sauce. Bring to the boil, cover, reduce the heat and simmer gently for 15 minutes, stirring occasionally.

Exchanges per serving:
Bread ¼
Fat 1½
Protein 3
Vegetable 1

STUFFED LAMB'S HEARTS
Serves 2 (225 Calories per serving)

Hearts are often neglected in cookery books but they have a good flavour and are well worth stuffing and stewing. They have a rather leathery texture so make sure they are cooked through.

2 × 4½-oz (135-g) lamb's hearts
1 teaspoon margarine
½ small onion, chopped
1oz (30g) fresh breadcrumbs
¼ teaspoon mixed herbs
1 tablespoon skimmed milk
5oz (150g) mixture of carrot, fennel and turnip
½ pint (300ml) vegetable or chicken stock
salt and pepper

① Wash the hearts, cut almost in half and remove any blood vessels or gristle, wash again.

② Melt the margarine over a moderate heat, add the onion and stir-fry 3–4 minutes.

③ Mix together the onion, breadcrumbs, herbs and sufficient milk to bind. Divide the stuffing between the hearts and tie firmly into their original shape with string.

④ Place the vegetables and hearts in a small casserole dish, pour over the stock and season with salt and pepper.

⑤ Bake at Gas Mark 4, 180°C, 350°F for 2¼–2½ hours.

> *Exchanges per serving:*
> Bread ½
> Fat ½
> Protein 2½
> Vegetable 1
> 5 Calories Optional Exchange

TRIPE AND ONIONS
Serves 2 (230 Calories per serving)

This is a traditional English recipe. The Protein Exchanges are correct as 10oz (300g) dressed tripe cooked in this way is reduced to only 7oz (210g) when cooked.

10oz (300g) dressed tripe
6oz (180g) onions, sliced
1 bay leaf
½ pint (300ml) skimmed milk
2 teaspoons margarine
4 teaspoons flour
salt and pepper
1 tablespoon chopped parsley

① Cut the tripe into large pieces, place in a saucepan with the onions, bay leaf and milk. Bring to the boil, cover, reduce the heat and simmer for about 1 hour until the tripe is soft when pierced with a knife.

② Drain the tripe, onions and bay leaf, reserve the liquor and discard the bay leaf.

③ Melt the margarine in a clean saucepan, add the flour, stir to mix and remove from the heat.

④ Gradually blend 6fl oz (180ml) of the cooking liquid into the flour. Season well with salt and pepper and bring to the boil, stirring all the time. Boil 1–2 minutes.

⑤ Stir the tripe and onions into the hot sauce and sprinkle with chopped parsley.

Exchanges per serving:

Fat 1

Milk ½

Protein 3½

Vegetable 1

20 Calories Optional Exchange

CUMIN CHICKEN
Serves 2 (190 Calories per serving)

Turkey fillets may be substituted for the chicken and additional vegetables such as sliced courgettes, bamboo shoots, bean shoots or sweetcorn added, but remember to add extra Exchanges.

2 teaspoons vegetable oil
¾ teaspoon cumin seeds
1 teaspoon finely chopped fresh root ginger
3oz (90g) drained canned water chestnuts, sliced
½ red pepper, cored and cut in strips
4 spring onions cut in 1-inch (2.5-cm) pieces
7oz (210g) chicken breast fillets, cut in ½-inch (1.25-cm) lengths
1 teaspoon flour
6 tablespoons chicken or vegetable stock

① Heat the oil in a saucepan, add the cumin seeds and stir round until they start popping.

② Add the ginger, water chestnuts, pepper, spring onions and chicken, stir round until the chicken loses its pink colour.

③ Sprinkle in the flour, stir and add the stock. Bring to the boil, reduce the heat, cover and simmer for 10 minutes.

Exchanges per serving:
Bread ½
Fat 1
Protein 3
Vegetable ½
15 Calories Optional Exchange

PEPPERED CHICKEN CASSEROLE

Serves 2 (270 Calories per serving)

If yellow peppers aren't available, use extra red and green peppers so the casserole remains colourful.

2 × 7-oz (210-g) chicken legs
2 teaspoons margarine
I onion, chopped
½ red pepper, cored and sliced
½ green pepper, cored and sliced
½ yellow pepper, cored and sliced
¼ teaspoon paprika
4 teaspoons flour
8fl oz (240ml) vegetable or chicken stock
salt and pepper

① Remove the skin from the chicken legs.

② Melt the margarine in a flameproof casserole dish. Turn the chicken legs in the hot fat to lightly brown. Remove from the dish.

③ Add the onions and peppers and stir-fry for 3–4 minutes over a moderate heat.

④ Stir in the paprika and flour and gradually blend in the stock. Bring to the boil, stirring all the time. Season to taste. Add the chicken and cover the casserole.

⑤ Bake at Gas Mark 4, 180°C, 350°F for about 35 minutes.

Exchanges per serving:

Fat I

Protein 3

Vegetable 1 ½

20 Calories Optional Exchange

CHICKEN AND RICE SALAD
Serves 2 (300 Calories per serving)

Serve this salad on its own or surrounded by a border of shredded lettuce and decorative radish roses. It makes an excellent packed lunch and can easily be transported in a plastic container.

2oz (60g) long grain rice
½ small red pepper, cored and diced
½ small green pepper, cored and diced
4 black olives, stoned and halved
2 spring onions, chopped
I small parsnip, diced
3oz (90g) fennel, chopped
5oz (150g) cooked chicken, cubed
For the dressing
2 teaspoons olive oil
2 tablespoons wine or cider vinegar
I clove garlic, crushed
salt and pepper
sprigs of watercress to garnish

① Cook the rice in boiling water according to the packaging instructions, drain.

② Mix together the rice, peppers, olives, spring onions, parsnip, fennel and chicken.

③ Place the oil, vinegar, garlic, salt and pepper in a small bowl and whisk together or place in a screw-top jar and shake to mix.

④ Pour the dressing over the rice mixture, toss well to mix.

⑤ Pile the salad onto a serving plate and garnish with sprigs of watercress.

Exchanges per serving:
Bread I
Fat I
Protein 2½
Vegetable 1½
10 Calories Optional Exchange

FRUIT AND CHICKEN SALAD
Serves 2 (235 Calories per serving)

This recipe can be made with either chicken or turkey and is an unusual way of using up leftovers. If fresh mandarins and pineapple aren't available, substitute 2oz (60g) drained canned mandarins and 4oz (120g) drained canned pineapple, but only use the varieties canned in natural juice.

1 medium mandarin
4oz (120g) fresh pineapple, core and peel removed
3oz (90g) black or white grapes or a mixture
8oz (240g) white cabbage, finely shredded
2 tablespoons chopped spring onions
5oz (150g) cooked chicken, cut in cubes
For the dressing
1 tablespoon low-calorie mayonnaise
5 tablespoons low-fat natural yogurt
salt and pepper
few Chinese cabbage or endive leaves to garnish

① Peel the mandarin, divide into segments and remove as much of the white pith from the segments as possible.

② Cut the pineapple into ½-inch (1.25-cm) cubes.

③ Halve and remove the seeds from the grapes.

④ Mix all the salad ingredients together in a bowl.

⑤ Pour the low-calorie mayonnaise into a small bowl, blend in the yogurt and season with salt and pepper, pour over the salad and toss to coat all the ingredients with the dressing.

⑥ Arrange the Chinese cabbage or endive leaves around the border of the serving plate or bowl. Pile the salad in the centre.

> **Exchanges per serving:**
> Fat ¾
> Fruit 1
> Milk ¼
> Protein 2½
> Vegetable 1½
> 15 Calories Optional Exchange

Fruit and Chicken Salad

TURKEY BALLS WITH SPINACH SAUCE

Serves 2 (195 Calories per serving)

If you prefer more highly seasoned food, add extra herbs or spices to the turkey balls. A few cumin seeds for example.

For the turkey balls
6oz (180g) turkey breast, minced
½oz (15g) fresh white breadcrumbs
½ teaspoon tarragon
finely grated zest of 1 lemon
1½–2 tablespoons beaten egg
salt and pepper
For the sauce
8oz (240g) spinach, roughly chopped
4 spring onions, chopped
3 tablespoons single cream
freshly grated nutmeg
salt and pepper

1. Mix the turkey, breadcrumbs, tarragon and lemon zest together. Add sufficient beaten egg to bind, season with salt and pepper.

2. Using damp hands, shape the turkey mixture into 8 balls.

3. Lay a small circle of non-stick baking parchment in a steamer, arrange the turkey balls on the paper and steam for 20–25 minutes.

4. Meanwhile, make the sauce. Wash the spinach well, shake off the excess water and place in a saucepan with the spring onions. Cover the saucepan and cook over a moderate heat for 4–5 minutes.

5. Tip the spinach and spring onions into a blender or food processor, process until it becomes a purée. Return the purée to the saucepan, stir in the cream and season well with salt, pepper and nutmeg, gently stirring all the time.

6. Serve the balls with the spinach sauce poured over the top.

Exchanges per serving:
Bread ¼
Protein 2½
Vegetable 1½
65 Calories Optional Exchange

QUAILS IN GRAPE SAUCE
Serves 2 (410 Calories per serving)

Quails are now readily available in supermarkets as well as at butchers. They only have a little meat so allow two quails per person.

4 × 4-oz (120-g) quails
1 tablespoon flour
salt and pepper
1 tablespoon vegetable oil
½ small onion, chopped
4 tablespoons chicken stock
6oz (180g) white grapes
1 teaspoon cornflour
1 teaspoon lemon juice
3 tablespoons soured cream

① Wipe the quails. Season the flour with salt and pepper. Coat each quail with the seasoned flour.

② Heat 2 teaspoons oil in a flameproof casserole, brown the quails all over, transfer to a plate.

③ Heat the remaining teaspoon of oil, add the onion and stir-fry for 3–4 minutes, add the stock and return the quails to the casserole. Cover and bake at Gas Mark 4, 180°C, 350°F for 30–40 minutes.

④ While the quails are cooking, put the grapes into a saucepan of boiling water, boil for 1–2 minutes, drain and slip off the skins. Halve the grapes and remove the seeds.

⑤ Transfer the quails to a warm plate. Blend the cornflour to a paste with the lemon juice and stock from the casserole, pour into the casserole, add the grapes and bring to the boil.

⑥ Stir the soured cream into the sauce and serve with the quails.

Exchanges per serving:
Fat 1 ½
Fruit 1
Protein 3
70 Calories Optional Exchange

RABBIT IN LEEK SAUCE
Serves 2 (285 Calories per serving)

To my surprise I found rabbit loin fillets in a local supermarket. I had intended to make a rabbit stew but decided to change my plans and this was the recipe I devised.

1 tablespoon margarine
9oz (270g) rabbit loin fillets, cut into thin strips
1 leek, thinly sliced
1 tablespoon flour
¼ pint (150ml) skimmed milk
2 teaspoons lemon juice
salt and pepper

① Heat 2 teaspoons margarine in a heavy-based saucepan, stir-fry the rabbit strips for about 5 minutes, remove from the pan.

② Heat the remaining teaspoon of margarine, add the leek and stir-fry 2–3 minutes. Sprinkle in the flour and mix well, gradually stir in the milk.

③ Bring to the boil, stirring all the time, add the rabbit, stir in the lemon juice, salt and pepper and simmer for about 4 minutes.

> *Exchanges per serving:*
> Fat 1 ½
> Milk ¼
> Protein 3 ½
> Vegetable 1
> 15 Calories Optional Exchange

FISH

There are many ways of classifying fish – freshwater or seawater, white fish which contain very little fat and oily fish which contain a high percentage of fat, or the structure of the fish, whether round or flat. I have decided to divide fish into only two categories: the first lists white and oily fish in alphabetical order for quick, easy reference and the second lists shellfish, also in alphabetical order. Following these lists, which include basic descriptions and methods of cooking, are separate sections illustrating what is meant by a fillet, cutlet etc. and how to prepare and cook fish.

Fish	Description	Preparation and Cooking
Anchovies	Very small sea fish, usually sold filleted, cured and packed in oil or brine, in bottles or cans.	Use only in small amounts as they are strongly flavoured and very salty. Traditionally used in Salad Niçoise and pizzas.
Bass	A sea fish, in season from May to August. Similar in shape to salmon.	Large bass may be sold in cutlets or steaks. They are suitable for poaching or baking. Small bass are usually grilled.
Bream	A sea fish in season from June to December. It is coarse-skinned with a white flesh and delicate flavour.	Bream can be cooked whole, stuffed and baked or sold in individual sized portions. It may be poached or grilled.
Brill	A flat sea fish in season all year round but claimed to be at its best between April and August. Its flavour and texture resembles turbot.	It is sold whole or cut into individual steaks. Poach, grill or bake. It may be served hot or cold.
Carp	A roundish flat freshwater fish in season between October and February.	This river fish often has a muddy flavour. It is advisable to soak it for about 3 hours in either salted water or water containing a little vinegar, then rinse well. Farmed carp doesn't require this preparation. Remove the scales if small, grill, but preferably stuff and bake or steam.

Cod

A large, round-bodied sea fish in season all year round but best between October and May. It has a firm white flesh. Also available salted.

Sold as fillets, cutlets or steaks. May be cooked in a variety of ways such as grilling, poaching, steaming on its own or sprinkled with herbs such as parsley, chervil or marjoram. Small cod or codling may be stuffed and baked whole.

Smoked Cod

Smoked cod fillets are pale yellow to deep golden yellow in colour, available throughout the year.

Poach or grill and serve alone, with a sauce or incorporated in fish pies etc.

Smoked Cod's Roe

A deep red brown colour, available throughout the year. It is sometimes possible to buy uncooked or boiled cod's roe.

Serve sliced as an appetiser with lemon wedges or use in place of grey mullet's roe in the traditional taramasalata.

Coley

A sea fish of the cod family. The greyish coloured flesh whitens during cooking. In season all year. A cheaper alternative to cod.

Usually sold as fillets. Ideal for soups, pies, stews. Use as for cod.

Conger Eel

A seawater fish, best during the autumn and winter months. The flesh is rather coarse but full of flavour. Also available smoked.

Eels may be baked, fried, stewed or jellied. Remove the skin before serving.

Dabs

Small sea fish of the plaice family. They are found in the mouth of estuaries. Dabs have a delicate flavour.

Sold whole or filleted. May be baked, grilled or fried.

Flounder

A flat-bodied sea fish in season from May to September. Similar to plaice in texture and flavour.

Cook whole or in fillets, either on their own or stuffed. Cook by steaming, grilling or baking.

HADDOCK

A round-bodied sea fish in season all year but at its best between September and February. It has a distinctive dark streak running down the back of the silvery skin and two black 'thumb marks' above the gills. It has a firm white flesh.

It is usually sold filleted but occasionally small whole haddocks are available. May be cooked in a variety of ways such as grilling, poaching, steaming on its own with a variety of herbs. It is also ideal for adding to fish pies etc.

Arbroath Smokies

This description includes small haddock or whiting which have been cleaned, soaked in brine, then hot smoked. They have had their heads removed and are often sold in pairs.

Often used as an appetiser. To cook, remove the skin, brush with margarine or oil then grill or bake. Ideal for adding to salads or dips.

Finnan Haddock	This haddock takes its name from Finnan in Scotland where the haddock was traditionally cured over peat smoke. The fish are headed, gutted and split down the backbone (but the bone is left in) then immersed in brine, threaded on spears and smoked. No dyes are used.	May be eaten on its own as it is bought, poached or added to Kedgeree, omelettes, etc.
Golden Cutlets	These are similar in appearance to Finnan haddock but the backbone is removed.	Cook and use in the same way as Finnan haddock.
Smoked Fillets	The bright yellow smoked haddock fillets are easily recognisable. Available all year.	Poach gently in milk or stock. Flake the fish and use with the milk or stock in pies or leave the fish whole and use the liquor to make a herb, cheese or an egg sauce. Traditionally used in Kedgeree.
Hake	A round-bodied sea fish of the cod family. In season all year round but at its best between June and January. The flesh is reasonably firm and with a good flavour. Hake is also available salted.	Usually sold as fillets, steaks or cutlets. May be grilled, baked or poached. Cold poached hake may be served with mayonnaise. Also used in pies and stews.
Halibut	A very large flat-bodied sea fish available all year round but at its best from August to April. It has a good flavour and firm flesh but tends to dry out during cooking. Greenland halibut and other varieties are also on sale.	Usually sold in steaks or cutlets. May be poached or baked. Use the poaching liquid in an accompanying sauce. If grilled it requires frequent basting to prevent drying out.
HERRING	A fairly small round-bodied sea fish. It is an oily fish with a creamy coloured flesh. Also sold salted.	Usually sold whole on the bone. Grill, bake or marinate and serve cold.
Bloaters	This process of preserving herrings was developed in Yarmouth during the 19th century. The whole fish are dry salted, washed, threaded on metal spears and smoked in kilns.	Usually poached or grilled. Can be made into paté with the addition of curd or cream cheese, lemon juice and a few fresh herbs.

Buckling	Usually headed and gutted, but the roe is left in, then soaked in brine and hot smoked. They have a delicate flavour.	As they are hot smoked they don't require further cooking. Serve cold either whole or skinned and filleted, or make into paté as described under 'bloaters'.
Kippers	Kippers are split and gutted by machine, soaked in brine then traditionally smoked over wood chips and sawdust. Dyes are sometimes now added. Often sold in pairs. A good kipper should be plump and juicy.	Either poach or grill and serve alone, or make into a paté or dip.
Roes	The soft roes have a creamy smooth texture and must be cooked within a day of purchase. A hard variety is available but difficult to obtain.	Sauté in margarine or oil, sprinkle liberally with lemon juice, salt and pepper.
Rollmops	The raw herring is headed, gutted, filleted and packed in brine and vinegar. Later the fillets are rolled and packed in jars with a spiced vinegar.	Serve uncooked with salads, as an appetiser or main course.
Huss	A sea fish, member of the shark family with firm pinky white flesh.	Usually sold filleted. Cut into pieces and use in stews or fish pies.

1   Crab
2   Cod fillet
3   Mackerel
4   Plaice
5   Sardines
6   Jumbo prawns
7   Peeled prawns
8   Salmon cutlet
9   Smoked salmon
10   Langoustine
11   Scallops
12   Red mullet
13   Mussels
14   Golden cutlets
15   Rainbow trout
16   Monkfish

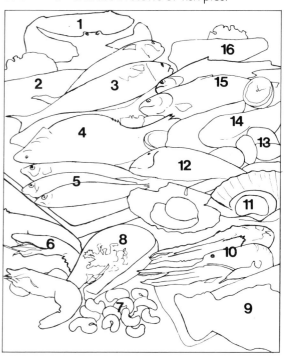

John Dory	A flat-bodied sea fish in season from October to December. Its body is almost oval in shape and has a firm white flesh with a good flavour.	Remove the head and fins and poach, bake or braise whole. Filleted John Dory may be steamed, baked or grilled.
Mackerel	A fairly small round-bodied sea fish in season from October to July but at its best from April to June. It has a blue-black glossy skin with cream coloured flesh and a distinct flavour.	Wash well and pat dry. Grill, bake or braise whole, or fillet and grill, bake or marinate and serve cold. Mackerel doesn't keep well so cook as soon as possible.
Smoked Mackerel	Hot and cold smoked mackerel as well as peppered smoked mackerel are sold.	May be eaten as purchased or grilled. Skinned and mixed with low fat soft, curd or cream cheese and herbs it makes a very tasty paté.
Monkfish	A deep-sea fish with a very ugly head which is generally removed before sale. The flesh is firm and white.	The whole tail may be braised or baked. Cut into slices or cubes it may be poached, stewed, grilled or barbecued. Also suitable for serving cold with mayonnaise.
Mullet, Grey	A round-bodied sea fish with a silvery skin, at its best between April and October. It has a good firm flesh. The smoked roe is used in taramasalata.	Cook whole by grilling, braising or baking. It may be stuffed, left on its own or sprinkled with herbs – sage is particularly good.
Mullet, Red	A round-bodied sea fish with a reddish skin which colours the flesh a white-pink. Smaller than grey mullet.	Cook as for grey mullet.
Pilchards	Small round-bodied sea fish with a silvery skin. The majority of pilchards are caught off the coasts of Devon and canned.	Brush with oil and grill.
Plaice	A flat-bodied sea fish with a soft white flesh and delicate flavour. In season all year but at its best at the end of May.	Cook whole or filleted. Remove the black skin from the fillets before serving. Cook by poaching, steaming, grilling, baking or braising.
Salmon	A prized freshwater fish which generally returns to coastal streams to spawn. Available all year round but British salmon is in season from February to August. There are three types of salmon, the most	Sold whole and in cuts from the middle of the fish or tail, or fillets. It is suitable for poaching, grilling or baking but requires basting to prevent it from drying out. Cold salmon is cooled in its cooking liquid,

highly sought after 'wild' salmon caught in British estuaries and rivers, 'farmed' salmon, and 'Canadian' salmon which has a coarser texture. The salmon roe is bright red and known as salmon caviar.

skinned and the fins removed, then served with mayonnaise.

Smoked Salmon

The fillets are dry salted, then cold smoked. It is sold whole or in bright pink wafer-thin slices.

Delicious on its own with a wedge of lemon. Requires no cooking, but make a simple dish like scrambled eggs extra special by adding a few trimmings of smoked salmon to it.

Salmon Trout

Often confused with salmon as it returns from the sea to spawn in coastal rivers. It is larger than a trout but smaller than a salmon, with a pale pink flesh. At its best during the summer months. Salmon trout is not available smoked.

May be cooked whole or in individual portions. Suitable for poaching, grilling or baking. Like salmon it has a tendency to dry out so requires frequent basting. May be prepared and served cold as for salmon.

Sardines

Small round-bodied oily seawater fish which are strictly speaking young pilchards, but the name is also given to young herrings and sprats when canned. Available fresh all year round. Sold fresh, smoked or canned.

Fresh sardines are usually cooked whole by grilling, baking or barbecuing.

Skate

A large flat-bodied sea fish. Only the 'wings' are eaten. It is at its best between October and April.

Poach, then serve with a hot sauce, or cool, remove the bone, flake the flesh and add to salads.

Sprats

A small round-bodied oily fish related to the herring. In season from November to March.

Wash the sprats and draw them through the gills. Barbecue, grill or bake whole fish.

Smoked Sprats

The sprats are washed, brined and smoked.

Remove the heads, then skin and fillet. This is rather fiddly and time-consuming. Serve cold or with salads.

Sole, Dover

This flat-bodied seawater fish is distinguished by its brownish black-grey skin. It has a firm, delicately flavoured flesh.

Cook whole or filleted. It is suitable for grilling, baking or steaming. The fillets may be grilled, steamed or lightly poached.

Sole, Lemon	Similar to Dover sole but without the distinctive dark skin. Although available all year round it is best from December to March.	Cook as for Dover sole.
Sturgeon	The fish is hard to obtain in this country although it is sometimes available during its season from August to March. The hard roe of various species of sturgeon is salted and known as caviar.	Caviar is an expensive delicacy. Serve ice cold with a little lemon. Usually eaten as an appetiser.
Trout	There are many varieties of this round-bodied freshwater fish. The most well known are the 'brown' and 'rainbow'. They are available all year round but at their best between April and August. The flesh is a very delicate pale pink.	Cook whole or filleted by poaching, steaming, grilling or baking. They are often stuffed before baking. Whole trout are served with their heads on. Cold trout should be skinned and filleted.
Smoked Trout	Usually rainbow trout which is gutted, the head left on, then hot smoked.	They require no further cooking. The delicate flavour only requires a squeeze of lemon. Serve on or off the bone.
Tuna	This round-bodied seawater fish is available fresh, sometimes called Tunny fish, but is better known as a canned fish.	The fresh tuna can be grilled, braised or baked.
Turbot	A flat-bodied sea fish in season all year but at its best from March to August. It has a creamy coloured moist flesh with an excellent flavour.	Usually sold in steaks and either poached, grilled or baked. Cold poached turbot is delicious skinned, boned and served with mayonnaise. Small turbot, or 'chicken turbot' as they are sometimes called, may be cooked whole by any of the methods given above.
Whitebait	Whitebait are tiny silvery seawater fish, in season all year but at their best from May to July. They are the silver fry of sprats and herring.	Usually left whole, not even gutted, and deep fried, but not particularly suitable if following a slimming diet.
Whiting	A round-bodied seawater fish related to cod. In season all year round but best from December to March.	Cook whole or in fillets. Poach, steam, grill, bake or add to pies etc.
Smoked Whiting	Sold as bright yellow fillets.	Use as for smoked cod or haddock.

Shellfish

The term shellfish covers a wide variety of fish without backbones or true skeletons. They form into two main categories: the 'crustacea' which include crabs, crayfish, lobsters, prawns and shrimps and 'molluscs' which have hard shells. There are two types of molluscs: those which live in a shell, for example cockles and winkles, and 'bivalves' which have two shells hinged together by a muscle such as oysters, mussels and scallops.

Shellfish	Description	Preparation and Cooking
Cockles	Cockles are molluscs about 1 inch (2.5cm) long. Unless bought by the sea they are sold cooked, shelled and either frozen or canned.	Use the cooked cockles in salads, soups and pasta or rice dishes.
Crabs	May be sold live or cooked. There are many species of these crustaceans. The cooked crabs may be sold whole or 'dressed'. The edible part of the crab consists of the white flesh from the claws and the brown meat which almost fills the shell. It is at its best between May and August. Also available canned.	The crab should be boiled if bought live. The white and brown meat may be included in seafood sauces or soups. It may be served with or incorporated in salads with a lemon or mayonnaise dressing.
Crawfish	These are clawless crustaceans, with most of their flesh in their tails. May be sold live or cooked. Unlike lobsters and crabs they don't turn bright red when cooked. Also sold canned.	Cook live crawfish by boiling or steaming. May be served hot, included in seafood sauces or cold with a simple salad dressing.
Crayfish	These crustaceans are often difficult to buy although they are in season from September to April. Crayfish resemble miniature lobsters. Sold live or cooked, they turn bright red when cooked.	If bought live, cook by boiling. Serve hot in a sauce or use as a garnish. Remove the meat from the shell and incorporate in or add to salads.
Langoustine	Also known as Dublin Bay Prawns or Scampi. They resemble tiny lobsters as they are crustaceans with elongated claws. They retain their pink colour when cooked.	Cooked langoustine may be served hot or cold. The majority of the meat is in the tail. Serve in salads or rice dishes.

Lobster

Lobsters are large crustaceans available all year round but at their best during the summer months. Sold live or cooked, when they turn bright red. Also available canned.

If bought live, cook by boiling. Serve hot in classic dishes such as Lobster Thermidor and seafood sauces or cold with a simple dressing.

Mussels

The molluscs must be bought live. The different species vary in appearance, but don't buy any mussel which has a gaping shell as the fish will be dead. Also sold canned.

Clean the shells with a stiff brush, pull off the 'beard' which sticks out of the shell, then wash again in cold water. Cook within a day of purchase. Place in a saucepan with a little liquid and shake occasionally. If the shells don't open, discard the mussel. Serve on their own or in soups, paella, etc.

Oysters

There are many species of these molluscs varying considerably in size, colour and flavour. They are in season from September to April. The shells must be firmly shut when bought. Also available canned.

Oysters may be served and eaten raw. They are traditionally added to steak and kidney pie and may be served in a cheese sauce or a variety of seafood dishes.

Prawns

These clawless crustaceans are usually sold cooked but may be purchased live. They turn pink when cooked. Fresh prawns are in season all year but at their best from February to October. Also available canned.

If bought live they should be boiled before use. Incorporate in salads, soups, pasta and rice dishes. Useful as a garnish when left unpeeled.

Scallops

Scallops are molluscs contained between two fluted shells. They are in season from October to March. The scallop should be white with a bright red roe attached.

Remove and discard the black vein and muscle from the side of the white flesh. Poach, grill or stir-fry the whole scallop. Detach the roe and add after 2 minutes of cooking. Cook for only 3–4 minutes altogether or they will become tough. Include in a seafood sauce or serve with a cheese sauce. Serve cold in or with a salad and simple dressing.

Scampi

These clawless crustaceans are usually sold cooked but are available live. Only the flesh in their tails is eaten. They resemble very large prawns.

Boil uncooked scampi and use in the same way as prawns.

Shrimps	Shrimps are small clawless crustaceans; usually sold cooked or in cans but available live.	Boil live shrimps. Use in sauces, chowders, pies and casseroles. Serve cold as for prawns.
Squid	Squid are of a rather unusual appearance; their limbs sprout from their head. Sold fresh, canned and smoked.	Pull off the head and tentacles, cut the head, leaving the tentacles whole. Pull out the transparent gristle from the body, wash the body sac well. Peel off any purple coloured skin from the outside of the body and leave whole or cut into thin rings. Stuff and bake whole in a sauce or poach. The rings can be poached or fried in a measured amount of oil.
Whelks	These are spiral-shelled molluscs up to 3 inches (7.5cm) long. Usually sold boiled but may be available uncooked.	If sold live, boil and remove the shell. May be sliced and stir-fried. Eat with a simple dressing or sauce.
Winkles	These small molluscs are usually sold boiled and shelled. Also available live or in brine.	Boil live winkles. Eat cold with a sprinkling of lemon juice or vinegar.

How to prepare fish

Always wash fish after purchase and store in a cool place, preferably the refrigerator. The method of preparation differs from one type of fish to another, but all fillets and cutlets only require rinsing and dabbing dry. Whole fish may need to be scaled, cleaned and skinned.

Scaling: Fish such as sea trout and salmon, which are served whole with their skin on, require scaling before cooking. Hold the fish under running water and run the back of a knife against the scales from the tail to the head until all the scales have been removed.

Cleaning a round fish: Slit along the abdomen of the fish from the gills to about halfway down the tail. Draw out the contents of the fish and rinse the fish to remove any blood. Rub a little salt inside, then rinse again to remove the black skin.

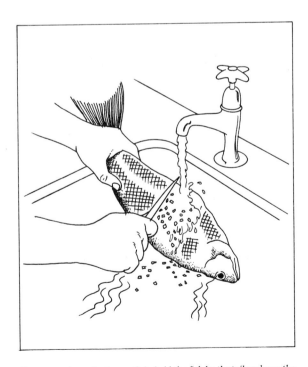

To remove the scales from a fish: hold the fish by the tail and run the back of a knife from the tail to the head. Rinse well.

Cleaning a flat fish: Open the cavity below the head under the gills. Draw out the entrails and clean as described above. Cut off the fins and gills. If the head is to be left on, remove the eyes, otherwise cut off the head and tail.

Skinning a round fish: This requires practice to do well. Using a very sharp knife, ease the point of the knife under the skin by the head and cut a narrow piece of skin away from the spine of the fish. Sprinkle your fingers with salt and gently but firmly pull the skin down from the head to the tail. Turn the fish over and repeat the procedure.

Skinning a whole flat fish: Cut off the fins. Only the dark skin of flat fish needs to be removed. Sprinkle your fingers with salt and hold the tail of the fish firmly while cutting across the skin just above the tail using a sawing motion and pressing the blade of the knife against the flesh. Continue the same motion up towards the head, gradually removing the skin but leaving the flesh intact.

Skinning a flat fish fillet: Lay the fillet skin-side down. Hold the tail with salted fingers. Cut under the flesh at the tail-end of the fish using a sawing motion. Continue the sawing motion upwards, keeping the blade of the knife as flat as possible against the skin. All skinning is far more easily carried out using a filleting knife which has a bendable sharp blade.

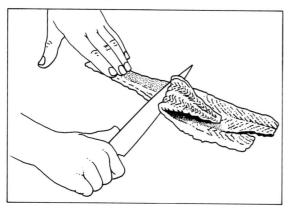

How to fillet fish

It is best to lay all fish which is to be filleted on a damp cloth and to use a very sharp knife, if possible a filleting knife.

Round-bodied fish: Remove the head. Keeping the knife blade flat, cut along the backbone as close to the bone as possible and using short, sharp movements. When the knife reaches the stomach, detach the fillet. Turn the fish over and repeat the procedure to obtain two fillets.

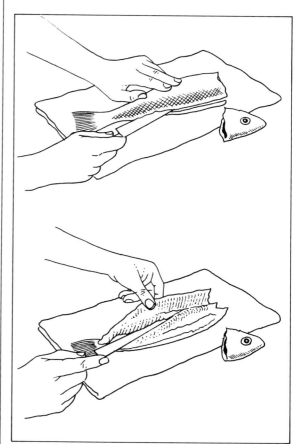

ABOVE
1. Remove the head and, keeping the knife blade flat, cut along the backbone using short, sharp movements.
2. Continue cutting until the knife reaches the stomach; detach the fillet.

LEFT
To skin a flat fish fillet: hold the tail end of the skin and, keeping the knife blade flat, use sawing motions to remove the flesh.

Soft-boned fish: Fish such as herring, mackerel and sprats are soft-boned and require special treatment. Cut off the head, tail and fins, cut along the whole length of the abdomen and clean as previously described. Lay the cut side down on the cloth and press firmly with your fingers from the head to the tail in one continuous movement. Repeat once more. Turn the fish over and lift the bone out leaving the flesh behind in one piece.

Flat fish: Cut off the fins but leave the tail and head attached. Using a sharp knife, slit from the head to the tail. Insert the knife under one side of the head and use smooth, definite strokes to remove the fish from the bones. Cut the fillet off at the tail end. Insert the knife under the other side of the head and repeat the procedure. Turn the fish over and remove two more fillets in the same manner. Four fillets are obtained from one flat fish.

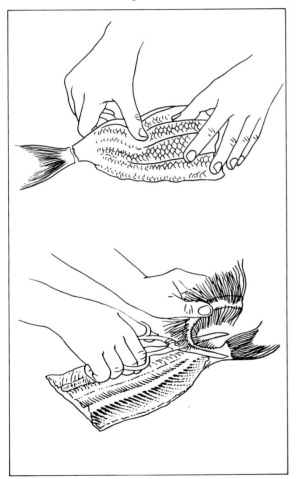

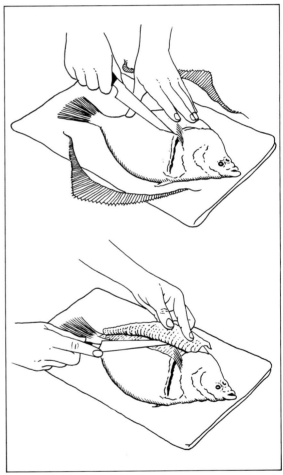

1. Press firmly on the skin side of the fillet from the top to the tail to loosen the bone.
2. Turn the fish over and ease out the bone, cut the bone from the tail with kitchen scissors.

1. Cut off the fins; slit from head to tail.
2. Insert the knife under one side of the head; use smooth cutting movements close to the bone to remove the fillet.

Cuts from a round fish

A large round fish may be sold filleted, as cutlets, steaks or as tail cuts. The fillets have been described above. The cutlets are taken from the head end of the fish. They are joined along the back of the fish but divide into two where the fish has been gutted. Steaks are cuts of fish taken from below the gutting cut and going towards the tail. Cutlets and steaks vary in width but are usually 1 inch (2.5cm) or more thick. The tail cut, as the name suggests, is the tail end of the fish.

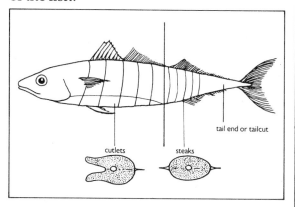

tail end or tailcut

cutlets   steaks

Methods of cooking fish

Poaching: Whole fish, fillets, steaks or cutlets may be cooked by this method. The poaching liquid is usually water for smoked fish but may be either milk, wine or stock for fresh fish. Cover the fish with the liquid, add any seasoning and bring slowly to the boil. Reduce the heat so it barely simmers and cook until the fish is tender. Allow approximately 10 minutes for every inch (2.5cm) of the thickest part of the fish, timing from when the liquor reaches boiling point. If the fish is to be served cold, leave to cool in the liquid. If a whole fish is to be boned or skinned, remove immediately, drain and carry out the necessary processes.

Steaming: All fish is suited to this method of cooking. Lightly grease the steamer and cook over simmering, not boiling water. To add extra flavour, sprinkle the fish with a little chopped chervil or tarragon and season with salt and pepper. Turn once during cooking. Wrap large fish in foil or baking parchment to retain the juices.

Frying: This is usually associated with large quantities of fat and the method is not suitable for anybody following a slimming diet. Most types of fish can be boned, cut into strips and stir-fried in a small measured amount of oil or margarine.

Braising: Whole fish, tailcuts or thick cutlets or steaks are suitable for braising. Lay the fish on a bed of lightly sautéed vegetables in a small amount of liquid, cover and cook on the hob or in a moderate oven.

Baking: Most fish can be baked, but foil or baking parchment should be used to wrap up the fish so it doesn't dry out during baking. Dot the fish with margarine or brush with oil and sprinkle with herbs and lemon juice, or stuff whole fish such as mackerel.

Grilling: Oily and white-fleshed fish are suitable for grilling, but it is worth marinading white fish in a mixture of oil and lemon juice before grilling to prevent them drying out. Also, the basting of all fish during grilling is important as the direct heat can cause even oily fish to become dry.

Barbecuing: Oily fish and the firm-fleshed white fish such as monkfish and grey mullet are suitable for barbecuing. The fish should be marinaded and continually basted as for grilling and only placed on the barbecue when the coals are glowing, not flaming.

PICKLED HERRINGS
Serves 2 (260 Calories per serving)

Pickled herrings are simple to make and are delicious with a salad as an appetiser or main course. They can easily be transported in plastic containers for picnics or packed lunches.

8oz (240g) herring fillets (3 or 4 fillets)
4fl oz (120ml) white wine vinegar
4 tablespoons water
6 white peppercorns
1 bay leaf
1 small onion, sliced

① Lay the herring fillets in an ovenproof dish.

② Pour over the vinegar and water. Add the peppercorns, bay leaf and onion slices. The liquid should cover the fish; if it doesn't, add a little extra vinegar.

③ Cover the dish with foil. Bake at Gas Mark 4, 180°C, 350°F for 25 minutes. Leave to cool in the liquid. Remove with a fish slice.

Exchanges per serving:
Protein 3

HERRING AND ORANGE SALAD

Serves I (280 Calories per serving)

This attractive salad tastes as good as it looks. The tangy orange combines well with the beetroot and herring. Use fresh beetroot, not the preserved beetroot which tastes strongly of vinegar.

4 or 5 small crisp lettuce or endive leaves
4oz (120g) beetroot, peeled
I medium seedless orange, peeled and pith removed
3oz (90g) spiced or soused mackerel fillets or pickled herrings (page 93)
I teaspoon chopped chives

① Arrange the lettuce or endive leaves round the edge of a round or oval serving plate.

② Thinly slice the beetroot and orange.

③ Place alternate slices of beetroot and orange in a circular or oval pattern round the plate.

④ Lay the mackerel fillets in the centre of the beetroot and orange, sprinkle with chopped chives and serve.

Exchanges per serving:
Fruit I
Protein 3
Vegetable 2

Herring and Orange Salad

STUFFED TROUT
Serves 2 (295 Calories per serving)

It's well worth looking out for the small trout. They are easy to prepare and can be just sprinkled with lemon juice and a few chopped herbs such as chervil or parsley, wrapped in foil and baked or stuffed as described below.

2 teaspoons margarine
1 shallot or ½ small onion, finely chopped
1½oz (45g) mushrooms, chopped
2 tablespoons chopped parsley
1¼ oz (35g) fresh breadcrumbs
1 tablespoon lemon juice
1 egg, beaten
salt and pepper
2 × 7-oz (210-g) trout, gutted but with heads on
lemon wedges to serve
sprigs of parsley to garnish

① Use a little of the margarine to grease a piece of foil large enough to hold the trout.

② Heat the remaining margarine in a saucepan, add the shallot and stir-fry 3–4 minutes, add the mushrooms and cook for a further 1–2 minutes.

③ Mix the parsley, breadcrumbs and lemon juice into the mixture, bind together with the beaten egg and

season with salt and pepper.

④ Wash the trout and dab dry with kitchen paper. Divide the stuffing between the two fish. Wrap loosely in foil and bake at Gas Mark 5, 190°C, 375°F for 20 minutes. The eyes of the trout will turn white when cooked.

⑤ Serve with lemon wedges and garnish with sprigs of parsley.

Exchanges per serving:

Bread ½

Fat 1

Protein 4

Vegetable ½

15 Calories Optional Exchange

MACKEREL WITH GOOSEBERRY SAUCE

Serves 2 (330 Calories per serving)

The sharp gooseberry sauce contrasts well with the oily mackerel. The amount of sugar required to sweeten the sauce will vary according to the sweetness of the gooseberries. Don't be tempted to add too much sugar or the sauce won't be sharp enough to complement the fish.

I teaspoon lemon juice
I teaspoon vegetable oil
2 × 7½-oz (225-g) mackerel, gutted but with heads on
salt and pepper
For the sauce
7½oz (225g) gooseberries, topped and tailed
½ teaspoon finely chopped fresh root ginger
5 tablespoons water
4 teaspoons sugar

① Mix together the lemon juice and vegetable oil.

② Make three diagonal slashes on each side of the mackerel. Season the fish with salt and pepper.

③ Lay the mackerel on the rack of the grill pan, brush with half the oil and lemon and grill for about 5 minutes under a moderate heat. Turn the mackerel, brush with the remaining oil and lemon, then return to the grill for a further 5 minutes.

④ Meanwhile place the gooseberries, ginger and water in a small saucepan, cover and simmer for 6–8 minutes until cooked.

⑤ Sieve the gooseberries. Return to the saucepan, add the sugar and stir until the sugar has dissolved and the sauce reaches boiling point.

⑥ Serve the mackerel with the gooseberry sauce.

Exchanges per serving:
Fat ½
Fruit ¾
Protein 4
40 Calories Optional Exchange

PACKAGED SALMON
Serves 2 (290 Calories per serving)

I don't think a recipe could be much simpler to prepare than this one, yet it retains the texture of the salmon, looks attractive and tastes delicious.

¼ teaspoon margarine
2 × 6-oz (180-g) salmon steaks
2 teaspoons chopped chervil
2 thin slices lemon
salt and pepper

① Lightly grease a piece of foil large enough to hold the salmon steaks with the margarine.

② Place the salmon steaks on the greased foil, sprinkle with the chervil and lay the lemon slices on top. Season with salt and pepper. Fold the foil over to form a parcel.

③ Bake in a preheated oven, Gas Mark 5, 190°C, 375°F, for 20 minutes.

Exchanges per serving:
Protein 5
15 Calories Optional Exchange

SMOTHERED FISH
Serves 2 (150 Calories per serving)

The combination of tomatoes, herbs and olives makes an interesting main course. For a change, substitute the oregano with 1–2 teaspoons freshly chopped chervil.

1 teaspoon olive oil
8oz (240g) whiting fillets
1 small onion, thinly sliced
½ green pepper, cored and cut into strips
1 clove garlic, finely chopped
¼ teaspoon oregano
¼ teaspoon basil
salt and pepper
4 black olives, stoned and halved
8oz (240g) tomatoes, peeled and sliced

1 Use a little of the oil to brush the base of an ovenproof dish, just long enough to hold the whiting, and about 2 inches (5cm) deep. Place the whiting in the dish.

2 Heat the remaining oil in a saucepan, add the onion, green pepper and garlic and stir-fry about 4 minutes.

3 Spread the onion, green pepper and garlic on top of the whiting, sprinkle with the herbs and a little salt and pepper. Add the olives.

4 Lay the tomato slices over the top, sprinkle with a little more salt and pepper, cover with foil and bake at Gas Mark 4, 180°C, 350°F for 35 minutes.

> Exchanges per serving:
> Fat ½
> Protein 3½
> Vegetable 2
> 10 Calories Optional Exchange

SMOKED WHITING IN LETTUCE LEAVES

Serves 2 (275 Calories per serving)

Take care not to overcook the lettuce; it only needs to be limp. This recipe can also be served cold with a lemon juice dressing – suitable as a starter for about 4 people.

2oz (60g) long grain rice
8oz (240g) smoked whiting fillets
1 teaspoon margarine
1 tablespoon spring onions
½ red pepper, cored and finely chopped
1 egg, beaten
salt and pepper
6–8 Cos lettuce leaves

① Prepare a steamer by laying a sheet of non-stick baking parchment over the base of the top half.

② Boil the rice according to the packaging instructions, drain.

③ Place the whiting in a pan, cover with cold water, heat gently and poach for about 8 minutes until cooked. Drain, remove the fish skin and flake the fish.

④ Melt the margarine in a small saucepan. Add the spring onions and red pepper, stir-fry for 4 minutes. Remove from the heat and stir in the cooked rice, fish, egg and seasonings.

⑤ Plunge the lettuce leaves in boiling water for about 1 minute until limp. Drain and spread out on a cooling rack.

⑥ Divide the whiting filling mixture between the lettuce leaves, fold the leaves over and roll up. Transfer to the steamer.

⑦ Steam the lettuce rolls for 20–25 minutes.

Exchanges per serving:
Bread 1
Fat ½
Protein 3
Vegetable 1

HALIBUT WITH LEEK AND MUSHROOM SAUCE
Serves 2 (330 Calories per serving)

It is worth re-weighing the halibut after poaching and removing the large central bone. I found the 5-oz (150-g) steaks weighed 3½oz (105g) when cooked and the bone was removed, but this will differ from one steak to another.

2 × 5-oz (150-g) halibut steaks
3oz (90g) leek, thinly sliced
1 tablespoon chopped parsley
6fl oz (180ml) skimmed milk
salt and pepper
4 teaspoons margarine
3oz (90g) button mushrooms, sliced
2 tablespoons flour

① Place the halibut steaks, leeks and parsley in a saucepan. Pour over the milk and sprinkle with salt and pepper. Heat gently until the milk begins to simmer, cover the saucepan and poach the halibut gently for 10–12 minutes until just cooked.

② Melt the margarine in a saucepan, add the mushrooms and stir-fry 2 minutes. Sprinkle in the flour, mix well and remove from the heat.

③ Remove the halibut from the milk etc. using a fish slice, remove the bones and transfer to a serving plate. Keep warm while completing the sauce.

④ Gradually blend the milk, leeks and parsley into the mushrooms. Bring to the boil stirring all the time. Boil 1–2 minutes. Adjust the seasoning and serve over the halibut.

Exchanges per serving:
Fat 2
Milk ¼
Protein 3½
Vegetable 1
35 Calories Optional Exchange

STEAMED FISH WITH VEGETABLES

Serves 2 (180 Calories per serving)

This simple dish requires only one saucepan and takes about 10–15 minutes to cook. Make your choice from cod, haddock or plaice.

2 teaspoons margarine
I leek, thinly sliced
I carrot, thinly sliced
I small courgette, thinly sliced
I tablespoon chopped chervil
5 tablespoons weak vegetable stock
2 × 5-oz (150-g) fillets cod, haddock or plaice
salt and pepper

① Melt the margarine in a saucepan, add the leek and stir-fry for 1 minute. Add the carrot, courgette, chervil and stock. Bring to the boil.

② Lay the fillets of fish on top of the vegetables, season with salt and pepper. Tightly cover the saucepan, reduce the heat and cook gently for 10–15 minutes, until the fish is just cooked.

Exchanges per serving:

Fat 1

Protein 4½

Vegetable 1½

ROLLED PLAICE FILLETS
Serves 2 (190 Calories per serving)

Serve these fillets with a selection of hot colourful vegetables to make a filling meal.

2 × 3½-oz (105-g) plaice fillets
1½oz (45g) prawns, roughly chopped
1oz (30g) fresh white breadcrumbs
1 tablespoon chopped parsley
1 tablespoon chopped chives
1 tablespoon finely grated Parmesan cheese
2–3 tablespoons skimmed milk
salt and pepper
½ teaspoon margarine
lemon wedges to serve

① Remove the skin from the plaice fillets.

② Mix together the prawns, breadcrumbs, herbs and cheese. Add sufficient milk to bind, and season with salt and pepper.

③ Spread the stuffing along the skinned side of the fillets, roll up and secure with cocktail sticks.

④ Use a little of the margarine to grease a small ovenproof dish just large enough to hold the fillets, dot the remaining margarine on top of the plaice and cover loosely with foil.

⑤ Bake at Gas Mark 4, 180°C, 350°F for 20 minutes. Serve with lemon wedges.

> *Exchanges per serving:*
> Bread ½
> Fat ¼
> Protein 3
> 30 Calories Optional Exchange

CHEESE-TOPPED COD
Serves 2 (145 Calories per serving)

This simple dish can be altered in a number of ways: either use a different fish such as haddock or plaice or replace the fennel with parsley or chervil.

2 × 3½-oz (105-g) cod fillets
½ teaspoon margarine
1 teaspoon chopped fennel
1oz (30g) cheese, grated
1 small tomato, sliced

1. Dot the skin-side of the fish fillets with margarine, grill for 4 minutes under a moderate heat.

2. Turn the fillets over, dot with any remaining margarine and grill for 2 minutes.

3. Sprinkle the fennel and cheese over the fillets, lay the tomato slices over each fillet and return to the grill for a further 2–3 minutes until the cheese has melted and is bubbling.

Exchanges per serving:
Fat ¼
Protein 3½
Vegetable ½

SMOKED SALMON ROLLS
Serves 2 (180 Calories per serving)

When you feel like spoiling yourself, this is the recipe to make. It can either be eaten by two people for lunch or supper or it may be served to four people as an appetiser.

3oz (90g) curd cheese
3oz (90g) cottage cheese
1 teaspoon lemon juice
2 teaspoons chopped chives
pepper
4 × 1-oz (30-g) thin slices smoked salmon
few lettuce or endive leaves
lemon slices to garnish

① Mix together the curd cheese, cottage cheese, lemon juice and chives, season with pepper.

② Lay the smoked salmon slices out and spread the cheese mixture over the length of each slice. Roll up 'Swiss roll' style.

③ Arrange the lettuce or endive leaves on the serving plates, transfer two salmon rolls to each plate and garnish with the lemon slices.

Exchanges per serving:
Protein 3½
Vegetable ½

CHEESE-TOPPED PIE
Serves 2 (345 Calories per serving)

This cheesy potato-topped pie is a meal in itself, but if you wish, serve additional hot vegetables such as green beans or courgettes.

½ teaspoon margarine
6oz (180g) smoked cod fillet
7fl oz (210ml) skimmed milk
9oz (270g) mixture of leek, carrot and calabrese broccoli
4 teaspoons cornflour
salt and pepper
For the topping
9oz (270g) potatoes
salt
3 tablespoons skimmed milk
1oz (30g) Double Gloucester cheese, grated

① Grease a deep 5-inch (12.5-cm) ovenproof dish with the margarine.

② Place the smoked cod fillet in a pan, pour over the milk. Cover and simmer very gently for about 10 minutes. Drain the fish, reserve the milk. Remove and discard the fish skin and flake the fish.

③ Thinly slice the leek and carrot. Thinly slice the broccoli stalk and divide the head into small florets.

④ Boil the prepared vegetables for 6 minutes, drain.

⑤ Blend the cornflour to a paste with a little of the reserved milk.

⑥ Mix the cornflour paste with the remaining milk, flaked fish and vegetables. Bring to the boil, stirring all the time. Boil 1–2 minutes. Season well. Transfer to the greased dish.

⑦ Boil the potatoes in salted water, drain and mash with the milk and cheese.

⑧ Spread the potato topping over the fish mixture, roughen with a fork and bake at Gas Mark 5, 190°C, 375°F for 15–20 minutes, or until the top is well browned.

Exchanges per serving:
Bread 1½
Fat ¼
Milk ¼
Protein 3
Vegetables 1½
45 Calories Optional Exchange

MONKFISH AND SCALLOP KEBABS

Serves 2 (145 Calories per serving)

Baste these kebabs frequently during cooking to prevent them drying out. Serve with plain boiled rice.

For the kebabs
4oz (120g) monkfish
4 scallops
½ green pepper, cored
3 button mushrooms, halved
2 spring onions, each cut into four pieces
2 small tomatoes, halved
For the marinade
1 tablespoon olive or vegetable oil
2 tablespoons lemon juice
½ teaspoon marjoram
½ teaspoon thyme
salt and pepper

① Cut the monkfish into four cubes. Place the monkfish and scallops into a dish.

② Whisk together all the marinade ingredients, pour over the fish and leave to marinate 1–2 hours.

③ Cut the green pepper into cubes, plunge into boiling water, boil for 3 minutes, drain.

④ Thread the monkfish, scallops, peppers, mushrooms and spring onions onto four skewers, ending with a tomato half.

⑤ Place the kebabs under a preheated grill, cook for 5–7 minutes, turning and basting frequently with the marinade.

Exchanges per serving:
Fat 1½
Protein 4
Vegetable 1¼

FISH CRUMBLE

Serves 2 (385 Calories per serving)

I've made this recipe with smoked cod, fresh cod and haddock and always been pleased with the flavour. Use whichever fish you prefer.

I clove garlic, finely chopped
I small onion, sliced
3oz (90g) fennel, chopped
I carrot, sliced
3oz (90g) green beans, sliced
I small can tomatoes
7oz (210g) smoked cod fillet
½ teaspoon basil
salt and pepper
I tablespoon cornflour
I tablespoon water
For the crumble
I oz (30g) wholemeal flour
I oz (30g) plain flour
4 teaspoons margarine
I oz (30g) mature Cheddar cheese, finely grated

① Place the garlic, onion, fennel, carrot, beans and tomatoes in a saucepan, stir round to break up the tomatoes.

② Remove the skin from the fish and cut in strips about 1½ inches (3.5cm) wide across the fillet, add to the saucepan with the basil. Season with salt and pepper.

③ Bring the tomatoes, fish etc. to the boil, cover, reduce the heat and simmer for 12 minutes.

④ Blend the cornflour to a paste with the water, stir into the fish mixture and bring to the boil, stirring all the time. Transfer the mixture to a deep ovenproof dish.

⑤ Make the crumble topping. Mix the two flours together, rub in the margarine until the mixture resembles fresh breadcrumbs, stir in the cheese.

⑥ Sprinkle the crumble over the fish base and bake at Gas Mark 4, 180°C, 350°F for 20–25 minutes.

Exchanges per serving:
Bread 1
Fat 2
Protein 3
Vegetable 3
15 Calories Optional Exchange

Fish Crumble

HOT SHERRIED PRAWNS
Serves 2 (160 Calories per serving)

Serve this dish with boiled rice and crisp lightly cooked broccoli to make a complete meal. Don't overcook the prawns as they shrink.

6oz (180g) peeled prawns
4 tablespoons dry or medium sherry
1 teaspoon finely chopped fresh root ginger
1 clove garlic, crushed
1 teaspoon vegetable oil
2 tablespoons chopped spring onion
3oz (90g) small courgettes, cut in thin strips
3oz (90g) bean sprouts
salt and pepper
1 tablespoon chopped coriander

1. Place the prawns in a dish, stir in the sherry, ginger and garlic and leave to marinate for about 2 hours.

2. Heat the oil, add the spring onion and courgettes and stir-fry for 2 minutes.

3. Pour the sherried prawns and the marinade into the courgettes, add the bean sprouts and stir over a moderate heat for 4–5 minutes. Season to taste and stir in the chopped coriander.

> *Exchanges per serving:*
> Fat ½
> Protein 3
> Vegetable 1
> 30 Calories Optional Exchange

KEDGEREE
Serves 2 (290 Calories per serving)

This is one of my favourite supper dishes. I prepare it in advance and heat it up when I arrive home. I also adapt the recipe to incorporate other ingredients I have in the cupboard, for example, red or green peppers.

6oz (180g) smoked haddock or cod fillets, skinned
3oz (90g) long grain brown rice
1 hard-boiled egg, chopped
4–6 spring onions, finely chopped
2 tablespoons chopped parsley
5 tablespoons low-fat natural yogurt
salt and pepper

① Lay the fish in a frying pan, cover with cold water and heat gently. Poach for about 10 minutes. Remove the fish from the water and flake with a fork.

② Boil the rice in the poaching water following the pack instructions and adding more water if necessary, for about 40 minutes.

③ Drain the rice if any liquid remains. Stir the flaked fish, egg, spring onions, parsley and yogurt into the rice and mix well. Heat gently, stirring all the time. Season well and serve.

> *Exchanges per serving:*
> Bread 1 ½
> Milk ¼
> Protein 3
> Vegetable ¼

PAELLA

Serves 2 (315 Calories per serving)

This traditional Spanish dish is a combination of various seafood and meat. If preferred use long grain brown rice but increase the boiling water by about 4 tablespoons.

2 teaspoons vegetable or olive oil
I clove garlic, finely chopped
I onion, chopped
I red pepper, cored and chopped
2 tomatoes, peeled and chopped
3oz (90g) long grain rice
good pinch of powdered saffron
7fl oz (210ml) water
juice of ½ lemon
salt and pepper
2oz (60g) cooked chicken, diced
2oz (60g) peeled prawns
4 unpeeled prawns
2 scallops
4 mussels, steamed
2 teaspoons chopped parsley
lemon wedges to garnish

① Heat the oil in a saucepan, add the garlic, onion and red pepper, stir-fry 3–4 minutes.

② Stir in the chopped tomatoes, rice, saffron, water and lemon juice, season with salt and pepper. Bring to the boil, stirring all the time, cover, reduce the heat and simmer for 12 minutes.

③ Add the chicken, prawns, scallops and mussels and stir over a moderate heat for a few minutes until the rice and scallops are cooked, the liquid absorbed, and the chicken and prawns heated through.

④ Transfer to a serving dish, sprinkle with parsley and garnish with lemon wedges.

Exchanges per serving:
Bread 1 ½
Fat 1
Protein 4
Vegetable 2

COD WITH PARSLEY SAUCE
Serves 2 (175 Calories per serving)

Serve this recipe with green beans and tomatoes which have been
halved, sprinkled with basil and grilled.

7oz (210g) cod
few rings of onion
½ bay leaf
¼ pint (150ml) skimmed milk
salt and pepper
2 teaspoons margarine
4 teaspoons flour
1 tablespoon chopped parsley

① Place the cod, onion rings and bay leaf in a saucepan, pour over the milk and sprinkle with salt and pepper. Cover the pan and simmer gently for 10 minutes.

② Melt the margarine in a saucepan, add the flour and remove from the heat.

③ When the fish is cooked, transfer to warm serving plates and keep warm while completing the sauce.

④ Strain the cooking liquid and gradually blend a little at a time into the margarine and flour.

⑤ Add the parsley and bring to the boil, stirring all the time. Boil 1–2 minutes, pour over the cod and serve.

Exchanges per serving:
Fat 1
Protein 3
20 Calories Optional Exchange

PEPPERED MACKEREL SALAD

Serves 2 (235 Calories per serving)

The peppered smoked mackerel fillets are available in many supermarkets. They are especially useful for packed lunches.

6½oz (195g) peppered smoked mackerel fillets
½ red pepper, cored and cut in strips
1 stick celery, chopped
2 tablespoons chopped spring onions
1½oz (45g) button mushrooms, sliced
1 crisp medium dessert apple, quartered, cored and cubed
2 tablespoons lemon juice

① Remove the skin from the peppered mackerel. Either flake the fish into large pieces or cut into chunks.

② Mix the red pepper, celery, spring onions, mushrooms and apple together.

③ Stir in the lemon juice and the mackerel.

Exchanges per serving:

Fruit ½

Protein 3

Vegetable 1

TUNA SALAD
Serves 2 (240 Calories per serving)

This pasta salad is simple to prepare and makes an attractive dish.

2oz (60g) pasta bows, shells or spirals
6 crisp lettuce leaves
6oz (180g) drained canned tuna in brine
½ red pepper, cored and finely chopped
2 tablespoons chopped spring onions
4 black olives, stoned and sliced
For the dressing
4 teaspoons low-calorie mayonnaise
1 tablespoon lemon juice
salt and pepper

① Boil the pasta according to the packaging instructions, drain well.

② Arrange the lettuce leaves round the edge of the serving bowl.

③ Flake the tuna, mix with the red pepper, onions, olives and pasta.

④ Measure the mayonnaise into a small bowl and very gradually add the lemon juice, mixing well after each addition. Pour over the tuna mixture and toss well to coat all the ingredients. Season well.

⑤ Pile the tuna salad in the bowl surrounded by lettuce leaves and serve.

Exchanges per serving:

Bread 1

Fat 1

Protein 3

Vegetable 1

10 Calories Optional Exchange

CRAB SALAD
Serves 2 (255 Calories per serving)

Assemble this salad just before serving so the colour of the beetroot doesn't have time to bleed over the other ingredients.

2 spring onions, finely chopped
few crisp lettuce leaves, shredded
I kiwi fruit
3oz (90g) freshly cooked small beetroots
½ red pepper, cored and chopped
2oz (60g) avocado, skinned and chopped
½ teaspoon lime juice
3oz (90g) white crab meat
3oz (90g) brown crab meat
For the dressing
2 teaspoons olive oil
2 tablespoons lime juice
pinch of powdered mustard
salt and pepper
few sprigs of watercress for garnish

① Mix together the spring onions and shredded lettuce, arrange round the edge of the serving plate.

② Peel and thinly slice the kiwi fruit. Thinly slice the beetroot. Arrange alternate slices of kiwi fruit and beetroot just inside the lettuce border.

③ Make a thin ring of red pepper beside the kiwi fruit and beetroot.

④ Mix the avocado and lime juice together with the white crab meat. Decoratively arrange the white and brown crab meat in the centre of the salad.

⑤ Place all the dressing ingredients in a small bowl and whisk together or pour into a screw-top jar and shake well to mix.

⑥ Trickle the dressing over the salad just before serving and garnish with sprigs of watercress.

Exchanges per serving:
Fat I
Fruit ½
Protein 3
Vegetable I
50 Calories Optional Exchange

KIPPER PATÉ
Serves 2 (155 Calories per serving)

This paté makes an ideal sandwich filling or can be divided in two and served with a salad to make a snack lunch. All the ingredients can be mixed in a blender or food processor if time is short, but I find the method given below gives a better texture.

4oz (120g) poached kipper fillets, weighed when skin and bones have been removed
2oz (60g) curd cheese
1 teaspoon chopped capers
2 teaspoons chopped chives
1 tablespoon lemon juice
salt and pepper
2 slices of lemon to garnish

① Mash the kipper fillets in a bowl.

② Mix in the curd cheese, capers, chives and lemon juice. Season to taste.

③ Divide the paté into two portions and either place in small ramekins or shape into a round. Pile in the centre of the serving plates so that salad can be arranged round the paté. Serve garnished with twists of lemon.

Exchanges per serving:
Protein 2½

VEGETABLES

Vegetables form an integral part of the Weight Watchers Food Plan. They add variety of flavour and texture as well as supplying essential nutrients and dietary fibre. By using a wide range of different vegetables, meals become increasingly appetising.

The following chart is a guide to help you choose good quality fresh produce and includes basic instructions for the preparation and cooking of individual vegetables.

Vegetable	Description	Preparation and Cooking
Akee	About 3 inches (7.5cm) long, red and open showing three black seeds. The creamy white edible part surrounds the seeds. Never buy over or under ripe akee which are poisonous.	Remove the red skin, pink tissue joining the seeds to the edible white part and the seeds. These are poisonous. Boil, sauté or stew the white part with fish or meat.
Alfalfa Sprouts	Very thin shoots about the thickness of mustard and cress with tiny yellow-green leaves. Do not buy wilting sprouts.	Wash well and incorporate in salads or sandwiches, or use as a garnish.
Artichokes, Globe	Choose evenly solid heads which feel heavy for their size. The leaves should be compact and the stem still attached. Do not buy soft or blemished vegetables.	Cut off the stalk and about 1 inch (2.5cm) from the top of the artichoke. Trim the spiny tips from each leaf with scissors. Spread the leaves out and, using a teaspoon,

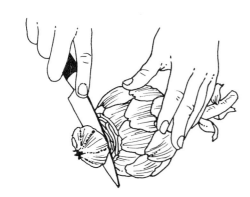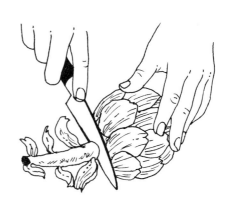

Artichoke, Globe
1. Cut about 1 inch (2.5 cm) off the top of the artichoke.
2. Remove the stalk from the base.

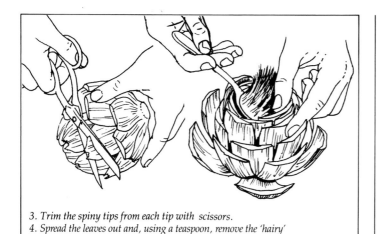

3. *Trim the spiny tips from each tip with scissors.*
4. *Spread the leaves out and, using a teaspoon, remove the 'hairy' choke.*

remove the 'hairy' choke. Soak in cold water with a tablespoon of lemon juice for about 45 minutes, then boil in salted water for 30–40 minutes or until a leaf can be easily pulled off. Drain upside down. To prepare the heart, remove the stalk and top of the artichoke, then continue removing leaves until only white-green leaves remain. Cut round the base of the artichoke in a spiral motion, removing the leaves to leave a smooth round white base. Place in cold water with a tablespoon of lemon juice until all hearts have been prepared. Boil for a few minutes in salted water.

| **Artichokes, Jerusalem** | The tubers vary according to variety in size and colour from beige to red-brown. Use only firm, unblemished tubers which feel heavy for their size. | Scrub or peel the tubers and serve grated or sliced in salads, bake whole or cut in pieces and boil in salted water. To prevent discolouration, keep the prepared vegetables in cold water. |
| **Asparagus** | Fresh asparagus is either white or green with tight compact tips and round spears. The stalks should be firm and tender, not fibrous or wilting. | Scrape off any outer scales, cut the asparagus all the same length. To cook whole, tie in bundles and boil upright in salted water, or steam. Alternatively, cut into diagonal slices, leave the tips whole, and sauté. |

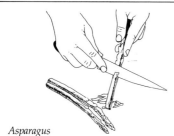  

Asparagus
1. *Scrape off the outer scales from the asparagus.*
2. *Cut all the asparagus the same length.*
3. *To cook whole tie in a bundle and cook upright in salted water, or steam.*

| **Aubergine** | Aubergines vary considerably in size, shape and colour from small and white to large and deep purple. All should have firm, smooth, glossy skins without blemishes or spongy areas. | Preparation and cooking varies according to variety, but the basic principles remain the same. Peel if desired, cut in pieces, sprinkle with salt and leave 30 minutes to allow the bitter juices to drain away. Rinse |

well then boil, steam, sauté, grill or bake.

BEANS
Broad

Firm, even-coloured green pods which vary in size from the small tender pods containing young beans to large fibrous pods, sometimes over 12 inches (30cm) long, containing large beans.

Very young pods may be topped and tailed and boiled whole in salted water. Remove the beans from older pods and then boil in salted water. For use in salads, slip the beans out of their waxy covering and toss in lemon juice.

Dwarf, French and Kenyan

Choose firm, crisp pods of an even green colour, about 6 inches (15cm) long. Do not buy blemished, wilted or fibrous pods.

Top and tail the pods and either cook in boiling salted water or steam. Cut in smaller pieces if desired before cooking.

Runner

The beans should be firm, straight and an even green colour. Older, larger beans tend to be fibrous. Do not buy wilting beans.

Very young beans may be cooked as dwarf beans. Remove the strings from the sides of older beans, cut in ½-inch (2.5-cm) strips or diagonal pieces. Boil in salted water.

Bean sprouts

White shoots, much thicker than alfalfa sprouts, with tiny yellow-green leaves. Only buy crisp beans with moist tops. The shorter beans are usually more tender.

Wash well and incorporate in salads or sandwiches or stir-fry.

Beetroot

Raw beetroot should be firm, smooth, round and deep red in colour. Do not buy very large, pitted or soft beetroot

Occasionally peeled, grated and eaten raw in salads. Usually scrubbed and boiled or baked. To boil, place in unsalted water, bring to the boil and simmer for 1–2 hours until the skin can easily be rubbed off. To bake, place in a preheated oven, Gas Mark 4, 180°C, 350°F and bake until tender.

BROCCOLI
Cape

Whole compact purple head surrounded by green leaves, resembling a cauliflower.

Remove the outer green leaves and cook whole or divide into florets. Cook in boiling salted water or steam.

Spears or Calabrese

The compact dark green heads should stand on firm stalks with a few fresh green leaves. Do not buy if the heads are open, yellowing or wilting.

Trim the toughest part of the stem. If the stem is over 1 inch (5cm) thick, make a few slashes through it to ensure even cooking. Boil in salted water or steam. Alternatively, cut in diagonal slices, divide into small florets and stir-fry.

Sprouting	The colour varies according to the variety, but usually purple or white heads on firm but tender stalks. Do not buy if the stalks are wilting.	Trim the ends of the stalks and boil in salted water or steam.
Brussels Sprouts	Choose small, firm, compact sprouts free from blemishes. Don't buy if they're soft, open or yellowing.	May be eaten sliced and raw in salads. To cook, remove any discoloured leaves, cut a cross in the stalk and boil in salted water or steam.

CABBAGE

Common Round (e.g. January King, Primo, Savoy)	The heads should be firm, heavy for their size and an even green colour, free from blemishes. Savoy are slightly soft with deeply marked leaves but the leaves should still be firm and crisp.	Cut in wedges or shred. Shredded cabbage may be eaten raw. To cook, boil in salted water or steam. For extra flavour either add a few caraway seeds when cooking or sprinkle with grated nutmeg after cooking.
Red	Choose firmly packed heads with crisp, glossy red leaves.	Prepare as for common cabbage and eat raw, boiled, steamed or pickled.
Spring Greens	These are semi-hearted cabbage with more open leaves than common cabbages. Do not buy if wilting or yellowing.	Cut off any thick bases from the leaves, shred and boil or steam as for common cabbage.
White	Choose firmly packed heads with fresh looking yellow-green leaves.	Shred and incorporate in salads or boil or steam as for common cabbage.
Carrots	Buy firm, well-shaped bright orange carrots. If the tops are attached they should be fresh.	Scrape or peel. Grate, slice or dice for use in salads. To cook, leave young carrots whole or slice, in lengths or rounds, and boil in salted water or steam.
Cauliflower	Buy compact, firm white heads surrounded by fresh green leaves.	Remove any coarse outer leaves and trim the stem. Break into florets to serve raw. Either leave whole and cut a cross in the base or divide into florets, then boil in salted water or steam. Sprinkle with nutmeg before serving for added flavour.

Celeriac

Choose firm, round celeriac with roots attached, about the size of a large orange. Larger vegetables tend to be 'woody'.

Peel thickly and leave in cold water with a tablespoon of lemon juice to prevent discolouration. Either grate and eat raw or cut in cubes and boil in salted water, steam or roast. Matchstick-sized pieces may be sautéed.

Celery

There are two main varieties and both should have crisp, ribbed stalks with leaves attached. The pascal or green celery has green stalks, the golden celery has almost white stalks with yellow-green leaves.

It is used as a vegetable and a herb. Serve raw either whole, diced or chopped. To cook, boil chunks of celery in salted water or steam. Alternatively, braise the whole trimmed head.

Chicory

Choose firm, crisp heads about 6 inches (15cm) long with tightly closed white leaves with yellow-green tips.

Trim the base and separate the leaves. Use whole or shredded in salads or as a garnish. Cook the whole heads in salted water, steam or braise.

Chinese Cabbage

Choose tightly packed heads composed of crisp light green leaves (resembles a cross between a cabbage and a lettuce).

Cut in pieces or shred and serve raw, or boil in salted water, steam or stir-fry.

Courgettes

The colour varies according to the variety but commercially available courgettes are usually deep to light green, but may be golden yellow. Buy firm, well rounded, unblemished courgettes, preferably small.

Courgette flowers may be used as a herb. Trim each end of the courgette, cut in strips, slices, dice or grate and use raw. To cook, leave whole or cut in pieces and boil in salted water, steam or stir-fry. May be stuffed and baked.

Cress

Sold in cartons, sometimes with mustard sprouts. The thin shoots are topped with tiny green leaves. Never buy wilting cress.

Cut above the level of the compost, wash and incorporate in salads or use as a garnish.

Cucumber

The size varies according to the variety but all should be firm, well shaped and an even green colour.

Trim the ends and slice, cut in strips, dice or grate to serve raw. Cut in thicker slices and boil briefly in salted water, steam or stir-fry. Serve sprinkled with lemon juice and chopped dill.

Endive	Buy clean, crisp, tightly packed curly leaves. The leaves vary in colour from yellow-green in the centre to dark green at the edge.	Trim the base and incorporate whole or shredded leaves in salads. To cook, cut in pieces and boil in salted water, steam or shred and stir-fry.
Fennel	The firm white-green ribbed bulbs should be crisp with a few feathery green leaves in the centre. Do not buy if the bases or stalks are turning brown.	The leaves are used as a herb and garnish. Trim the stem and remove any coarse leaves, shred and incorporate in salads. Leave whole, halve, quarter or cut in pieces and boil in salted water, steam or braise.
Garlic	Buy firm, plump bulbs composed of several cloves with clean unbroken papery skins.	Use in small quantities. Peel and either rub round a salad bowl or crush or chop and add to salads. Use whole or chopped in soups, stews etc. If used whole, remove before serving the dish. Chop or slice and add to stir-fries.

How to crush a clove of garlic:
1. Choose a plump bulb of garlic.
2. Pull out a clove and remove its papery skin.
3. Place the clove of garlic in the press and squeeze to extract the juice.

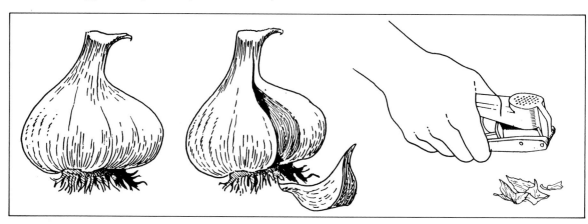

Grape Leaves	Rarely sold fresh but should be an even green colour	Blanch the fresh leaves in salted water before stuffing then boil, steam, braise or bake.
Kale	The leaves should be crisp and dark green with a frilly edge. Do not buy if wilting or bruised.	Remove thick mid-ribs and any tough leaves. Cut large leaves into pieces and boil in salted water.
Kohlrabi	Varies according to variety, either green or purple. Buy small kohlrabi with fresh tops. Large heads tend to be woody.	The bulb and leaves may be eaten. Cut off the stems and chop. Remove and wash the leaves and cook separately or with the bulb. Peel the kohlrabi unless very young, slice, cut in strips or dice and add to salads or boil in salted water or steam.

Lamb's Lettuce	Choose 4–6-inch (10–15-cm) tall stems with green even coloured leaves. Depending on the variety the leaves are either round with a smooth edge or uneven and in tight rosettes. Only buy very fresh produce.	Wash well and incorporate the leaves in salads or wash, shake and place in a covered saucepan with a little salt and no additional water. Boil briefly.
Leeks	Buy leeks composed of compact leaves, white near the base and roots and bright green at the top.	Cut off the roots and coarse upper part of leaves. Wash very well, several times. Shred or thinly slice if serving raw. Cook whole, halved or sliced leeks in boiling salted water, steam or braise.
Lettuce	There are numerous varieties on sale which differ considerably in size and colour. All should be fresh, crisp and a good colour whether green, yellow-green or red. Avoid blemished, bruised or wilting leaves.	Lettuce is usually washed, and whole, torn or shredded leaves incorporated in salads. Some lettuce with a strong flavour e.g. Cos, make delicious soups and purées. They may also be stuffed whole, or as individual leaves, and steamed or braised.
Marrow	The size and colour depends on the variety. Some are deep green and others have pale yellow-green stripes. All should be firm and glossy with unblemished skins.	Trim both ends, leave the skin on. Halve, remove the seeds, stuff and either bake or steam. Alternatively slice or dice, remove the seeds and boil in salted water or steam. If preferred the seeds may be removed after cooking.
Mushrooms	The size and shape varies from the tiny, closed cap white button mushroom to the large open cap showing brown gills. All skins should be firm and free from wrinkles and blemishes.	Wipe, no need to peel. Either slice and serve raw or leave whole, halved, sliced or diced and add to stews, soups and stir-fries. Large mushrooms may be stuffed and baked.
Okra	Buy young, tender, crisp green pods free from blemishes. Pods over 3 inches (7.5cm) tend to be fibrous.	Trim off the stem ends, leave small pods whole, cut larger pods in half. Boil in salted water or add to soups and stews where they will act as a thickener.

Onions

The size and flavour varies considerably according to the variety. Red and white skinned onions tend to be mild but the brown skinned varieties may be mild or very strong. All should be firm with papery dry skins free from blemishes.

Remove the skin and slice or grate mild onions for use in salads. To cook, leave whole, halve, slice or dice and boil in salted water, steam, stir-fry or add to casseroles, soups etc. May be stuffed and baked or left whole and braised.

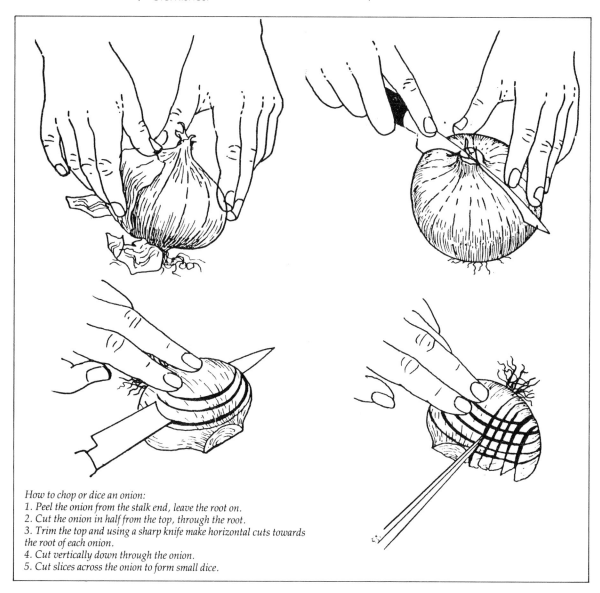

How to chop or dice an onion:
1. Peel the onion from the stalk end, leave the root on.
2. Cut the onion in half from the top, through the root.
3. Trim the top and using a sharp knife make horizontal cuts towards the root of each onion.
4. Cut vertically down through the onion.
5. Cut slices across the onion to form small dice.

Parsnips

Choose small to medium parsnips; large ones tend to be woody. They should be firm and fairly clean. Avoid soft, blemished or wrinkled produce.

Scrape or peel. Leave whole, cut in half lengthwise, strips, slices or dice. Boil in salted water or steam. Whole, halved or quartered parsnips may be roasted.

PEAS
Garden

Choose well filled, large bright green pods. Do not buy yellowing or wet ones.

Shell the peas; young ones can be eaten raw. To cook, boil in salted water or steam. Serve sprinkled with chopped mint, chives or basil.

Mangetout

The flat, crisp bright green pod should be tender and the tiny seeds contained in the pod just visible through the skin.

Top and tail the pods and cook very briefly by boiling in salted water, steaming or stir-frying.

Sugar or Snow

Similar to mangetout but the tapering pods contain slightly larger seeds or peas.

Cook as for mangetout.

PEPPERS
Bell

Available in a number of colours: white, yellow, mauve or the more common red and green. Do not buy blemished or wrinkled produce.

Remove core and seeds. Slice, dice or cut in strips and eat raw or add to casseroles and stir-fries or stuff and bake. To remove the skins, place under a hot grill and turn until evenly charred, plunge into cold water then slip off skin. This gives a slightly smoky flavour.

Chilli

Many varieties are available differing in shape, colour and pungency. Do not buy wilting or blemished chillies.

Handle with care; do not rub eyes or allow the chilli to come into contact with broken skin as it will burn and cause irritation. Remove the stalks but the seeds may be eaten. Finely chop and use sparingly either raw or added to stews, casseroles, stir-fries etc.

Potatoes

The size and colour varies according to the variety but choose fairly clean, smooth and well shaped produce free from green patches. Do not buy blemished or sprouting potatoes.

New potatoes may be scrubbed and boiled in salted water with a sprig of mint. Older potatoes may be scrubbed or peeled and cooked in the same way or scrubbed, pricked with a fork and baked. They may also be sliced, diced or cut into strips and sautéed or halved and roasted.

Sweet Potatoes

These are larger than ordinary potatoes and almost oblong in shape. The most common variety is red-brown in colour and often has a few roots attached. Choose only firm, unblemished produce.

Scrub and boil, steam, bake or roast as for potatoes.

Pumpkin	Buy clean pumpkins with a firm rind and bright orange in colour without blemishes. If bought in wedges, check the flesh is not beginning to rot or the rind to crack.	Cut the pumpkin in half and remove the pulp and seeds. To boil or steam, cut into small pieces and peel, cook then drain and mash with salt and pepper. To bake, place the cut pieces in a pan, brush with margarine and bake until tender.
Radicchio	Choose small, round-hearted radicchio with deep red leaves and white veining free from bruising. Do not buy wilting or open produce.	Wash, separate the leaves and use whole or shredded in salads or as a garnish.
RADISHES **Common Red**	If possible avoid topped radishes sold in plastic bags. Buy medium-sized, smooth, bright red round or oval radishes with fresh green tops.	Remove all leaves and roots. Leave whole, halve or slice and serve raw or cut into decorative shapes and leave in cold water to open before use. May be sliced and added to stir-fries.
Daikon and White	These radishes should both be clean, firm and a creamy white colour. The Daikon is a long and a cylindrical shape; the White is shaped like a parsnip, wide at one end and tapering to a point.	Peel and slice thinly or grate and incorporate in salads. To cook, peel, slice thinly and add to soups, stews or stir-fries.

1   Endive
2   Cabbage
3   Peppers – bell
4   Kohlrabi
5   Courgettes
6   Onions
7   Turnip
8   Scorzonera
9   Baby sweetcorn
10   Kenyan beans
11   Alfalfa sprouts
12   Carrots
13   Brussels sprouts
14   Parsnip
15   Swede
16   Aubergine
17   Radish
18   Asparagus
19   Chicory
20   Cauliflower
21   Globe artichoke
22   Radicchio
23   Mushrooms
24   Jerusalem artichokes
25   Okra
26   Tomato
27   Sweet potato

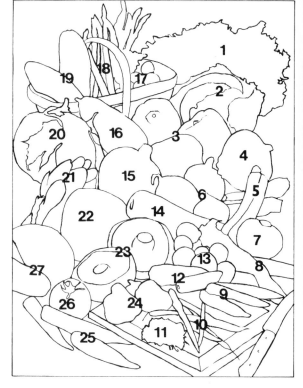

Salsify and Scorzonera	Salsify should be a grey-white colour, firm and the thin root should taper at one end. Scorzonera or Black salsify is similar in size and shape but has a black skin covering the white flesh.	Trim and scrape the root, place in cold water with a tablespoon of lemon juice to prevent discolouration while preparing the rest of the salsify. Cut into 2-inch (5-cm) lengths and boil in salted water with a little lemon juice or vinegar. May also be sautéed.
Shallots	Choose firm, rounded dry shallots with the brown papery skin intact.	Use in the same way as onions.
Sorrel	There are many varieties of sorrel but all leaves should be bright green and crisp without blemishes or woody stems. The smaller and fresher the sorrel the better the flavour.	Wash the leaves, remove any tough stalks and cut or shred before adding to salads. May be boiled or steamed and puréed, sautéed or added to soups.
Spinach	Choose fresh dark green, crisp flat or crinkled leaves. Avoid long stems and wilting or yellowing leaves.	Use only very small tender leaves in salads. To cook, cut off hard stalks and slice large leaves; wash well, drain, place in a covered pan and boil without additional water.
Spring Onions	Buy clean spring onions with round or oval bulbs and fresh bright green tops. Avoid soft spring onions with wilting leaves.	Trim, wash and leave whole, halve, slice or chop and incorporate in salads. To cook, leave whole or halve and boil briefly in salted water. Use the chopped green part of the leaves as a garnish.
Swedes	Buy smooth, round or oblong, firm swedes which feel heavy for their size.	Peel and cut into cubes, slices or matchstick-sized pieces. Boil in salted water or steam.
Sweetcorn	Whole cobs should have bright yellow kernels which are plump, firm and tightly packed. The kernels should be surrounded by silky threads covered by green husks.	Remove the outer husk and silky threads, trim the ends. Boil in unsalted water with a little lemon juice. To remove the kernels from the cobs, slice along the cob with a knife. The cob may also be roasted but the silky threads must be removed and the green husks tied back over the kernels.
Baby Sweetcorn	Very small bright yellow cobs about 3 inches (7.5cm) in length and tapering to a point. Do not buy wilting or discoloured produce.	To cook, boil or steam.

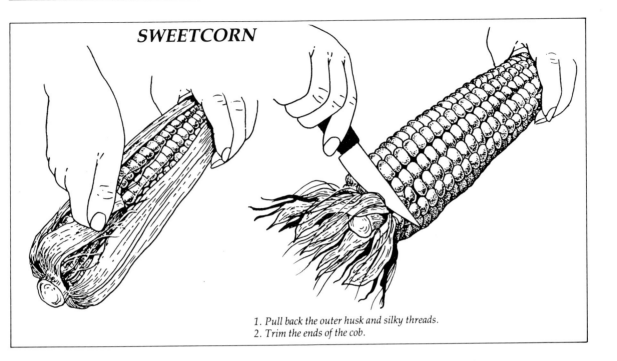

SWEETCORN

1. Pull back the outer husk and silky threads.
2. Trim the ends of the cob.

Swiss Chard	Fresh crisp dark green leaves with prominent white veins and thick white stems. Avoid wilting or blemished produce.	The stems and mid-ribs may be cooked as one vegetable and the leaves as another. Cut the stems into pieces, add the mid-ribs and boil in salted water with a little lemon juice. Treat the green leaf as for spinach. Whole leaves with the mid-ribs may be cooked in boiling salted water.
Tomatoes	Buy firm, well formed bright red tomatoes, with a fresh open calyx on top. The more shrivelled the calyx the greater the length of time since it was picked.	Serve whole, quartered or sliced in salads or as a garnish. Halve and sprinkle with basil or leave whole and grill or bake. To remove tomato skins, plunge in boiling water for 20–30 seconds, dip in cold water then slip off the skins.
Beefsteak Tomatoes	Use the same guidelines as for tomatoes, but as beefsteak tomatoes are so much larger, check there are no splits in the skin or soft patches.	Use as for tomatoes or halve, remove the seeds, stuff and bake.
Cherry Tomatoes	Buy small, even-sized, round firm tomatoes with open calyces.	Use as for tomatoes but particularly useful as a garnish.

Truffles

Vary in colour according to variety. Both black and white varieties have powerful scents when fresh. They are irregularly shaped with a warty skin and solid flesh.

Slice thinly, dice, grate or cut in thin strips and incorporate in salads or add to dishes towards the end of the cooking time.

Turnips

Many varieties are available. The most common is white at the base and turns green at the top. They should be firm, either round or slightly elongated. Avoid large blemished produce with wilting tops.

Peel, slice thinly, dice or grate and incorporate in salads. Young turnips should be peeled and cooked whole or cut in pieces and boiled in salted water, steamed or added to casseroles etc. Large turnips can be left unpeeled and baked. Matchstick-sized pieces can be stir-fried.

Watercress

Choose bright green leaves on crisp stems. Do not buy wilting or yellowing watercress.

Wash well and add to salads or use as a garnish. To cook, boil in salted water or steam. Delicious in soups.

Yams

Buy firm, oblong-shaped yams without blemishes or soft spots.

Cook as for potatoes or sweet potatoes.

CRUNCHY BEETROOT SALAD
Serves 2 (115 Calories per serving)

Beetroot and orange has always been one of my favourite combinations but the addition of apple and celery gives an interesting variety of textures as well as colours. Don't use beetroot which has been preserved in vinegar, only freshly cooked beetroot.

4oz (120g) cooked beetroot
1 medium seedless orange
1 medium dessert apple
1 stick celery, thickly chopped
1 small head of chicory
For the dressing
4 teaspoons lemon juice
2 teaspoons olive oil
pinch of mustard powder
1 tablespoon chopped chives
salt and pepper

1. Remove the skin from the beetroot, cut into ½-inch (1-cm) cubes.

2. Using a sharp knife, cut the peel and white pith from the orange. Slice the orange, cut each slice into quarters.

3. Quarter the apple, remove the core. Cut the apple into ½-inch (1-cm) cubes.

4. Mix the beetroot, orange, apple and celery together.

5. Divide the head of chicory into leaves and arrange round the edge of the serving dish.

6. Place all the dressing ingredients into a screw-top jar, shake well to mix.

7. Pour the dressing over the beetroot etc. and toss well. Pile into the serving dish.

Exchanges per serving:
Fat 1
Fruit 1
Vegetable 1½

VEGETARIAN CRUMBLE
Serves 2 (370 Calories per serving)

Remember the tip of storing measured quantities of margarine in the freezer. It makes the task of rubbing in so much cleaner and quicker. This makes a delicious supper dish for a cold winter's night.

I clove garlic
I small onion, sliced
I large stick celery, chopped
2oz (60g) mushrooms, quartered
3oz (90g) swede, cut in chunks
3oz (90g) carrots, sliced
6oz (180g) cooked kidney beans
7fl oz (210ml) vegetable stock
2 tablespoons tomato purée
½ teaspoon mixed herbs
For the crumble topping
Ioz (30g) wholemeal flour
Ioz (30g) medium oatmeal
4 teaspoons margarine
Ioz (30g) Cheddar cheese, finely grated

① Place the garlic, onion, celery, mushrooms, swede, carrots, kidney beans, stock, tomato purée and herbs in a deep flameproof casserole, no more than 6½ inches (16cm) in diameter.

② Cover the casserole and simmer gently for 10 minutes.

③ Meanwhile, prepare the crumble.

Mix the flour and oatmeal together. Rub the margarine into this mixture until it resembles fresh breadcrumbs. Stir in the cheese.

④ Remove the lid from the casserole, sprinkle the crumble evenly over the top and place in a preheated oven Gas Mark 4, 180°C, 350°F. Bake for 15–20 minutes.

Exchanges per serving:
Bread 1
Fat 2
Protein 1½
Vegetable 2½
10 Calories Optional Exchange

SIMPLE COLESLAW
Serves 2 (105 Calories per serving)

This crunchy salad is quick and simple to make. It keeps well if covered and stored in the refrigerator.

4oz (120g) white cabbage, finely shredded
3oz (90g) carrots, finely shredded or grated
1 stick celery, finely chopped
½ green pepper, cored and thinly sliced
1 tablespoon chopped spring onions
1oz (30g) sultanas or raisins
a few radicchio or lettuce leaves
For the dressing
2 tablespoons low-calorie mayonnaise
2 teaspoons lemon juice
½ teaspoon caraway seeds
salt and pepper

① Mix the cabbage, carrots, celery, green pepper, spring onions and sultanas together.

② Arrange the radicchio or lettuce leaves round the edge of the serving dish.

③ Stir the dressing ingredients together, pour over the cabbage etc. and toss well to coat all the vegetables.

④ Pile the coleslaw in the centre of the radicchio or lettuce leaves.

Exchanges per serving:
Fat 1 ½
Fruit ½
Vegetable 2

CARROT AND ORANGE SOUP
Serves 2 (55 Calories per serving)

I find the sweetness of carrots is complemented by the tang of oranges. If you enjoy this soup, try the same combination as a salad using grated carrots and an orange juice dressing.

I medium leek, thinly sliced
10oz (300g) carrots, chopped
12fl oz (360ml) vegetable stock
good pinch of thyme
juice of ½ an orange
salt and pepper

① Reserve a few slices of leek, place the remainder in a saucepan with the carrots, stock and thyme. Bring to the boil, reduce the heat, cover and simmer for 30 minutes.

② Transfer the vegetables and stock to a blender or food processor and process until smooth.

③ Return the purée to the saucepan, add the orange juice and season well. Stir over a moderate heat, pour into warm serving bowls and garnish with the reserved leek separated into rings.

> *Exchanges per serving:*
> Vegetable 2½
> 15 Calories Optional Exchange

SWEDE AND CARROT PURÉE
Serves 2 (55 Calories per serving)

I've always enjoyed mashed swede as a vegetable accompaniment to meat and fish dishes but this version using half quantities of swede and carrot tastes excellent.

6oz (180g) swede, cubed
6oz (180g) carrot, cubed
salt
1 teaspoon margarine
freshly grated nutmeg
pepper

① Boil the swede and carrot in salted water for 10–15 minutes until tender, drain.

② Transfer the vegetables to a blender or food processor, add the margarine, nutmeg and pepper and process until smooth.

③ Adjust the seasoning and serve piping hot.

Exchanges per serving:
Fat ½
Vegetable 2

ARTICHOKE SOUP
Serves 2 (100 Calories per serving)

Many years ago a friend invited me to supper and made a soup similar to this one. She made me guess what the ingredients were – I identified the artichokes but not the apple. I often wished I'd asked her for the recipe but made this one up in an attempt to re-create her dish.

I small clove garlic, finely chopped
12oz (360g) Jerusalem artichokes, sliced
I small onion, chopped
I medium cooking apple, cored and chopped
½ pint (300ml) vegetable stock
¼ pint (150ml) skimmed milk
salt and pepper
1–2 teaspoons finely chopped parsley to garnish

① Place the garlic, artichokes, onion, apple and stock in a saucepan. Bring to the boil, reduce the heat, cover and simmer 20–25 minutes.

② Transfer the vegetables etc. to a blender or food processor and process until smooth.

③ Return the purée to the saucepan, stir in the milk and season to taste. Reheat the soup, pour into large warm soup bowls and serve sprinkled with chopped parsley.

Exchanges per serving:
Fruit ½
Milk ¼
Vegetable 2½

RATATOUILLE

Serves 2 (110 Calories per serving)

This colourful dish is suitable for a midday meal or supper. It can be cooked in the oven or simmered gently on the hob for 30–40 minutes.

6oz (180g) aubergine, cubed
salt
2 teaspoons vegetable or olive oil
1 clove garlic, finely chopped
1 small onion, chopped
1 small green, red or yellow pepper (or a mixture), seeded and sliced
6oz (180g) courgettes, thickly sliced
1 small can tomatoes
1 tablespoon tomato purée
½ teaspoon dried basil or 2 teaspoons chopped fresh basil
2 teaspoons chopped parsley or sprig of basil to garnish (optional)

1. Sprinkle the aubergine with salt, leave to drain 20–30 minutes then rinse well and pat dry.

2. Heat the oil in a flameproof casserole. Add the garlic, onion and pepper and sauté 2–3 minutes.

3. Mix in the courgettes, tomatoes, tomato purée and basil. Stir round to break up the tomatoes.

4. Cover the casserole and place in a preheated oven, Gas Mark 4, 180°C, 350°F for 45 minutes. Serve sprinkled with chopped parsley or garnished with a sprig of fresh basil.

Exchanges per serving:

Fat 1

Vegetable 4

5 Calories Optional Exchange

BROAD BEAN SALAD
Serves 2 (155 Calories per serving)

This salad can easily be transported in a plastic container and taken to work for lunch. Make it the night before it is to be eaten, and store in the refrigerator.

1 red pepper
6oz (180g) shelled broad beans
4oz (120g) peeled prawns
For the dressing
2 tablespoons lemon juice
2 teaspoons olive oil
1 tablespoon chopped chives
1/4 teaspoon French mustard
salt and pepper
lemon wedges to serve

① Grill the pepper until blistered and black, turning occasionally, plunge in cold water. Remove the skin and core and cut the flesh into small dice.

② Boil the broad beans for about 6 minutes (if using frozen beans reduce the time to 2 minutes), plunge into cold water and pop each bean out of its waxy skin.

③ Mix the chopped pepper, beans and prawns together in a bowl.

④ Place all the dressing ingredients in a small bowl and whisk together or put into a screw-top jar and shake well.

⑤ Pour the dressing over the salad, toss and serve with lemon wedges.

Exchanges per serving:
Fat 1
Protein 2
Vegetable 1 1/2

VEGETABLE CURRY
Serves 2 (105 Calories per serving)

This recipe makes a delicious curry which can be eaten as a snack or made into a more substantial meal by adding 6oz (180g) drained, cooked kidney or butter beans with the cauliflower etc. This of course will add 1 Protein Exchange per serving.

10oz (300g) mixture of vegetables chosen from the following: cauliflower, turnip, swede, parsnip
2 teaspoons vegetable oil
1 clove garlic, finely chopped
½ small chilli, seeded and finely chopped
¼ teaspoon cumin seeds
¼ teaspoon ground coriander
¼ teaspoon turmeric
1 teaspoon finely chopped ginger
1 small onion, chopped
2oz (60g) okra, halved
2 tablespoons tomato purée
½ pint (300ml) vegetable stock

① Break the cauliflower into florets, cut the turnip, swede and parsnip into 1-inch (2.5-cm) cubes.

② Heat the oil in a saucepan. Add the garlic, chilli and spices, stir over a moderate heat for 1–2 minutes.

③ Add all the remaining ingredients, mix well and bring to the boil. Cover the saucepan and simmer for 15 minutes. Remove the saucepan lid and simmer for a further 10 minutes.

> *Exchanges per serving:*
> Fat 1
> Vegetable 2½
> 10 Calories Optional Exchange

STIR-FRIED VEGETABLES
Serves 2 (120 Calories per serving)

This quick recipe retains the flavour and texture of the vegetables. Sliced leeks, courgettes or celery can always be added or used to substitute for the beans and carrot.

1 tablespoon vegetable oil
1 teaspoon finely chopped fresh root ginger
1 clove garlic, finely chopped
½ red pepper, cored and cut in strips
4–6 spring onions, cut in thick diagonal slices
2oz (60g) green beans, cut in 1-inch (2.5-cm) pieces
1 carrot, cut in thin strips
3oz (90g) beansprouts
2 teaspoons soy sauce
1 tablespoon tomato purée
3 tablespoons water
4 teaspoons sherry
salt and pepper
½ teaspoon sesame seeds, toasted

① Heat the oil in a saucepan. Add the ginger and garlic and stir-fry for 1–2 minutes. Mix in all the remaining vegetables and stir-fry for a further 3 minutes.

② Mix the soy sauce, tomato purée, water and sherry together, pour over the vegetables and stir well.

③ Cover the saucepan and simmer for 6 minutes. Adjust the seasoning and transfer to a warm serving dish, sprinkle with sesame seeds and serve immediately.

Exchanges per serving:
Fat 1 ½
Vegetable 2
20 Calories Optional Exchange

Stir-Fried Vegetables

HOT MANGETOUT SALAD
Serves 2 (60 Calories per serving)

As the name 'mangetout' implies, the peas are just topped and tailed and then everything is eaten. This method of cooking retains the flavour and crisp texture of the peas.

2 teaspoons olive oil
I teaspoon finely chopped fresh root ginger
4oz (120g) mangetout, topped and tailed
½ red pepper, seeded and cut into thin strips
I tablespoon red wine vinegar
salt and pepper

① Heat the oil, add the ginger and stir-fry for 1 minute.

② Mix in the mangetout and stir-fry for 2 minutes.

③ Add the pepper and vinegar and cook for a further 1–2 minutes stirring all the time. Season with salt and pepper. Serve immediately.

Exchanges per serving:
Fat I
Vegetable I

CREAMY SPINACH SALAD
Serves 2 (65 Calories per serving)

Only use very small young spinach leaves which are absolutely fresh for this recipe. The older leaves are far too tough and would ruin the salad.

2oz (60g) young spinach leaves
2oz (60g) Chinese cabbage, shredded
2oz (60g) button mushrooms, sliced
For the dressing
½ teaspoon coriander seeds
pinch mild chilli powder
1 tablespoon cream cheese
5 tablespoons low-fat natural yogurt

① Tear or cut the spinach leaves in half. Mix together with the Chinese cabbage and mushrooms.

② Roughly crush the coriander seeds in a small bowl using the back of a teaspoon or end of a rolling pin. Add the chilli powder and cream cheese, gradually mix in the yogurt a tablespoon at a time.

③ Pour the dressing over the salad and toss well. Leave in the cool for about an hour for the dressing flavours to be absorbed.

Exchanges per serving:
Milk ¼
Vegetable 1
50 Calories Optional Exchange

BAKED COURGETTES
Serves 2 (240 Calories per serving)

I use a mature Cheddar cheese in this recipe but a mixture of Parmesan and Cheddar would work equally well.

2 × 3–3½-oz (90–105-g) courgettes
2 teaspoons margarine
3 tablespoons chopped spring onions
2oz (60g) mushrooms, chopped
1½oz (45g) mature Cheddar cheese, finely grated
1½oz (45g) fresh wholemeal breadcrumbs
1 egg, beaten
1 tablespoon chopped chervil
salt and pepper

① Boil the courgettes for 5–6 minutes, drain. Cut in half lengthways and scoop out the inner pulp leaving the skin intact. Chop the pulp.

② Melt the margarine, sauté the spring onions and mushrooms for 1–2 minutes.

③ Reserve a little cheese for sprinkling over the top. Add the remainder to the mushrooms.

Stir in the breadcrumbs, egg, chopped courgette pulp and chervil. Season well.

④ Spoon the stuffing into the four courgette halves. Line a baking sheet with foil, lay the courgettes on the foil and fold loosely over. Bake in a preheated oven, Gas Mark 4, 180°C, 350°F for 25–30 minutes. Unwrap the foil for the last few minutes of baking.

Exchanges per serving:

Bread ¾

Fat 1

Protein 1¼

Vegetable 1½

TOMATO SAUCE
Makes approximately 1 pint (600ml). Serves 5 (20 Calories per serving)

Although this recipe can be halved I find it easier to make up at least 1 pint (600ml) and freeze it in 4-fl oz (120-ml) quantities. It is useful as an accompaniment to grilled fish or meats and especially good in casseroles and stews.

1 lb (480g) tomatoes, quartered
½ small onion, chopped
1 carrot, chopped
1 stick celery (including leaves), chopped
½ teaspoon sugar
sprig of basil
salt and pepper

① Place all the ingredients in a saucepan, cover and heat very gently. Simmer for 45–50 minutes.

② Transfer the tomatoes etc. to a blender or food processor. Blend for a few seconds, then sieve to remove the tomato seeds, skin etc.

③ Adjust the seasoning and either use at once or store in 4-fl oz (120-ml) quantities.

Exchanges per serving:
Vegetable 1 ½
5 Calories Optional Exchange

BRUSSELS SPROUT PURÉE
Serves 2 (120 Calories per serving)

Brussels sprouts are usually boiled or steamed and served as a whole vegetable. This purée makes a change; it retains the strong, distinctive sprout flavour but has a pretty green colour and smooth texture. About 1lb (480g) of brussels sprouts as they are bought will yield the amount required when they've been trimmed.

14oz (420g) brussels sprouts
1 shallot or ½ a small onion, chopped
salt
1 teaspoon margarine
3 tablespoons single cream
1–2 teaspoons lemon juice
freshly grated nutmeg
pepper

① Boil the brussels sprouts with the shallot or onion in salted water for about 10 minutes. Drain and reserve the boiling liquid.

② Transfer the brussels sprouts and onion to a blender or food processor, add the margarine and cream and process until smooth.

③ Add lemon juice, nutmeg, salt and pepper to taste and process for a further few seconds. If necessary add a little of the reserved cooking liquid to achieve the correct consistency.

④ Reheat the purée, stirring all the time.

> *Exchanges per serving:*
> Fat ½
> Vegetable 2½
> 50 Calories Optional Exchange

SWEET AND SOUR VEGETABLES

Serves 2 (130 Calories per serving)

These vegetables are an ideal accompaniment for grilled fish or meat. Don't overcook the vegetables or they will lose their crisp texture.

15oz (450g) mixed vegetables selected from: parsnip, swede, carrot, turnip, dwarf beans and cauliflower florets
1 teaspoon vegetable oil
1 clove garlic, finely chopped
1 teaspoon finely chopped fresh root ginger
1 small onion, chopped
1 tablespoon tomato purée
¼ pint (150ml) vegetable stock
1 tablespoon cornflour
4 teaspoons soy sauce
2 tablespoons wine or cider vinegar
4 tablespoons orange juice
1 teaspoon sugar
salt and pepper
sprigs of coriander to garnish

① Prepare the vegetables. Cut the parsnip, swede, carrot and turnip into sticks about 1½ inches × ¼ inch (3 × 0.5cm). Cut the beans into 1-inch (2.5-cm) lengths, divide the cauliflower into small florets and chop the stalk.

② Heat the oil in a saucepan. Add the garlic, ginger and onion and stir-fry for 3 minutes.

③ Stir in the remaining vegetables, tomato purée and stock. Bring to the boil, cover, reduce the heat and simmer for 8 minutes.

④ Blend the cornflour and soy sauce together, add the vinegar, orange juice and sugar. Stir the cornflour mixture into the vegetables, bring to the boil, stirring all the time, season with salt and pepper. Boil 1–2 minutes.

⑤ Serve the vegetables garnished with sprigs of coriander.

Exchanges per serving:
Fat ½
Vegetable 3
45 Calories Optional Exchange

MIXED SALAD WITH BLUE CHEESE DRESSING

Serves 2 (160 Calories per serving)

The blue cheese dressing makes almost any salad more tasty and enjoyable. Serve the salad and the dressing separately.

6 radicchio leaves
½ red or yellow pepper, cored and cut in half rings
1 stick celery, chopped
1 tablespoon spring onions, chopped
4 endive leaves
1 medium seedless orange
For the dressing
2oz (60g) blue cheese such as Gorgonzola or Danish Blue
1 teaspoon olive oil
2–3 tablespoons cider or white wine vinegar
salt and pepper

① Place the radicchio leaves, pepper, celery and spring onions in a salad bowl.

② Tear the endive leaves into pieces and add to the salad.

③ Using a sharp knife, cut the peel and pith off the orange, cut in half lengthways, then slice. Mix into the salad.

④ Make the dressing. Grate the cheese into a small bowl, mash with a fork and gradually add the oil and vinegar. Season to taste.

⑤ Serve the salad and dressing separately. Spoon the dressing over the salad just before eating.

Exchanges per serving:
Fat ½
Fruit ½
Protein 1
Vegetable 1¼

MIXED BEAN SALAD
Serves 2 (195 Calories per serving)

The time dried beans take to cook varies considerably, but always boil hard for at least 10 minutes, then continue over a moderate heat. Never add salt to the water as it will toughen the bean skin and considerably increase the cooking time.

3oz (90g) selection of dried beans, for example: kidney, haricot, flageolet and butter beans
3oz (90g) shelled broad beans
3oz (90g) green beans, cut in 1-inch (2.5-cm) lengths
For the dressing
2 teaspoons olive oil
2 tablespoons wine vinegar
1 tablespoon tomato purée
salt and pepper

① Cover the dried beans with cold water and leave to soak several hours or overnight.

② Drain the dried beans, cover with cold water and boil fiercely for 10 minutes, reduce the heat and continue boiling until cooked, about 2 hours, drain.

③ Boil the broad beans and green beans for 6 minutes (if using frozen broad and green beans boil for only 2 minutes). Pop the broad beans out of their waxy skins.

④ Mix all the warm drained beans together.

⑤ Place all the dressing ingredients in a small bowl and whisk together or put into a screw-top jar and shake well.

⑥ Pour the dressing over the salad, toss and leave to cool.

Exchanges per serving:

Fat 1

Protein 1 ½

Vegetable 1

5 Calories Optional Exchange

GREEN CHEESE SALAD

Serves 2 (225 Calories per serving)

So many think of a green salad as a few lettuce leaves, slices of cucumber and celery. This salad uses a wider selection of more interesting flavours and textures and incorporates a small amount of cheese to make it more substantial. I prefer the salad without a dressing but add one if you wish.

½ small green pepper, cored and chopped
2oz (60g) Chinese cabbage, shredded
1 small courgette, sliced
1oz (30g) bean sprouts
2oz (60g) drained sliced bamboo shoots
1 tablespoon chopped spring onions
3oz (90g) white grapes, halved and seeded
few sprigs of watercress
3oz (90g) Caerphilly cheese

① Mix the green pepper, Chinese cabbage, courgette, bean sprouts, bamboo shoots, spring onions and grapes together in a bowl.

② Cut the cheese into small cubes.

③ Add the cheese to the salad and toss well.

Exchanges per serving:
Fruit ½
Protein 1½
Vegetable 1½

FRUIT

With such a wide range of fruit on sale, it is important to be able to recognise good-quality produce. It's only too easy to be tricked by a 'ready to eat' sign on a papaya or a mango and then find it's as hard as a rock.

As the Weight Watchers Food Plan includes a considerable variety of fruit, it's important to include many different kinds in sweet and savoury recipes so your diet remains varied and interesting. The chart below is a guide to help you choose good-quality fresh fruit and includes basic preparation and cooking instructions. It's impossible to mention every available fruit but I hope the following will be a useful guide.

Fruit	Description	Preparation and Cooking
APPLES Cooking	Many varieties are available, but probably the most well known is the English Bramley. It should have a green smooth skin free from bruises and blemishes.	They may be stewed and incorporated in crumbles, topped with meringue etc. To bake, remove the core, score the skin round the centre, stuff and bake in a moderate oven. Apple sauce is the traditional accompaniment to pork. They are also preserved in chutneys, jams and jellies. All apples – cooking, crab and dessert – turn brown when peeled. To prevent discolouration, either turn in lemon juice or place in a bowl of water containing 2 tablespoons of lemon juice.
Crab	These are very small, sour apples with shiny firm red or yellow skins.	Mainly used in jam and jelly making as they have a high pectin content, necessary for setting jams.
Dessert	There are a number of different dessert apples available, varying in colour from the brown-green Russet to the bright red Worcester Pearmain. All should have smooth unblemished skins.	Usually eaten raw, alone or in fruit or savoury salads.

Apricots	The fruits should be round, about the size of a plum with a slightly velvety textured skin. They should be orange-coloured and sometimes have a slight blush. Avoid very hard fruits which are under-ripe, and very soft fruits which are over-ripe as the texture of the flesh will be spoilt. They should just feel soft when gently pressed.	Eat raw or cooked. Raw, they may be eaten alone or incorporated in fruit or savoury salads. Stewed, they are added to crumbles etc. They may also be made into jams or chutneys. It is worth breaking a few apricot stones and removing the kernels to add to the fruit when cooking as they give a delicate almond flavour.
Bananas	Bananas are imported green and gradually ripen to yellow. The ripe fruit has brown speckles on the skin – don't mistake bruises for these. Don't store in the refrigerator or they will turn black.	Eat raw or cooked. As bananas discolour quickly after peeling, turn in lemon juice to keep the pale yellow colour of the flesh. Eat alone or in sweet or savoury salads. Stew and use in a variety of desserts or savoury dishes, particularly with chicken.

BERRIES

Blackberries	The fresher the blackberry the shinier the fruit. Choose plump shiny fruit, almost black in colour.	Eat raw or cooked. They are frequently used with apples in pies, crumbles etc. but may be stewed and puréed and made into sorbets. They are also made into jams and jellies.
Blueberries	The dark purple skin is almost black. The berries should be round with a smooth skin and definite bloom. They are larger than blackcurrants and may reach ½ inch (1.25 cm) in diameter.	Eat raw or cooked. They may be stewed and used in many desserts or sauces, pickled or made into jam or wine.
Cranberries	The colour varies from yellow-red to crimson according to the variety. All the berries are about ½ inch (1.25 cm) in diameter and should have firm smooth skins.	The skins are tough and the white flesh sour so stew without sugar until the skins pop. Don't overcook or they will taste bitter. Sweeten after stewing. May be used in desserts or made into sauces or jellies to accompany meat or game.
Gooseberries, Cape	Cape gooseberries are difficult to obtain in this country. The ripe berry is encased in an orange-yellow lantern-shaped case.	Particularly useful as a garnish. They may be eaten raw, stewed or made into jam or jelly.

Gooseberries, Common	The colour ranges from red to yellow/green according to the variety. The skin should be firm and smooth.	Before use, top and tail each gooseberry. They may be stewed and used in desserts or puréed and used in sweet recipes or to accompany fish, particularly mackerel.
Loganberries	They are similar in shape but larger than raspberries, with a harder central hull. Their colour varies from dark red to almost purple.	Eat raw or cooked. They add flavour and colour to fresh fruit salads but may be stewed and used in many desserts.
Mulberries	They should be a little larger than blackberries and have a deep purple, firm flesh.	Eat raw or cooked. Often used with apples and served as desserts or made into jams or jellies.
Raspberries	Choose undamaged red berries. Don't buy fruit which has been bruised and look out for juice at the bottom of boxes of prepacked raspberries. This indicates damaged fruit.	Eat raw or cooked. Remove the central hull and eat alone or in fruit salads. They may be stewed and used in a variety of desserts, made into purées or sauces. They are also used in jam making.
Strawberries	The small wild strawberries have a wonderful flavour but aren't available commercially. The English strawberry is red and heart shaped. Imported varieties tend to be larger and of uneven shape. Never buy blemished or bruised fruits.	Eat raw or cooked. Remove the central hull and serve alone or with other fresh fruits, or stew and incorporate in a wide variety of desserts. Strawberry purée forms the basis for sorbets, sauces and fools etc. They are also used in jam making but require lemon juice or additional pectin.
Cherries	The colour varies according to the variety from yellow-red to almost black. They should be firm, plump and shiny. The dark Morello cherries are only suitable for cooking.	Eat raw or cooked. They may be used whole or stoned in fruit salads, stewed, added to pies or a variety of desserts. They are also used in jam making, when it is advisable to crack some of the stones and extract the kernels to add extra flavour.

Extract the stones from the cherries, then crack each stone to extract the kernels.

CURRANTS

Blackcurrants

Choose currants which are small but plump with a slight bloom. Don't buy soft currants.

Usually stewed and included in a wide variety of desserts. Also used in jam and jelly making and the juice is used to make blackcurrant cordial.

Redcurrants

The berries should be brilliant red and firm. They are often sold in clusters on long stalks.

Usually stewed and included in a wide variety of desserts. Frequently puréed and the pips discarded. Redcurrants are used in jelly making.

Whitecurrants

The berries are similar to redcurrants, although white in colour, and sold in clusters on long stalks.

Use as for redcurrants.

Damsons

A small plum with a blue-purple skin. They should be slightly soft to touch but not blemished or bruised.

Unless absolutely ripe, the damson can be very sour. They are usually stewed and incorporated in a wide variety of desserts or made into jam or jelly.

Dates

These oval fruits are about 1 inch (2.5 cm) in diameter and 1½–2 inches (4–5 cm) long. They should have very dark brown shiny skins which are paper-like and tough. Don't buy dates with broken or damaged skins.

Eat raw or cooked. Dates may be eaten on their own or stoned and stuffed. Because of their high sugar content they may be incorporated with other fruits to help sweeten them: for example to stuff baked apples. They are also used to make chutneys.

Figs

There are many varieties of figs varying from a small pear shape to an egg shape, and the colour from black, to white or gold, brown or green. The two varieties most widely available are the green-skinned figs with a yellow-green flesh and the blue-purple skin with a reddish flesh. Figs are easily damaged when ripe so check they aren't bruised.

Fresh figs are usually eaten raw, either alone or with Parma ham. They may be stuffed with cottage, cream or curd cheese. They are used to make liqueurs and may be used in pickling.

Grapefruit

There are two main types of grapefruit on sale: the 'white' which has a yellow skin and the 'red' which has a pink-tinged skin. The sizes vary from the size of a large orange upwards. Don't buy fruit with damaged skins.

Eat raw or cooked. Raw, they may be peeled and divided into segments to serve on their own or in fruit salads, or halved and the flesh loosened with a grapefruit knife or serrated knife and then divided into segments for easy

(Grapefruit continued)

eating. They may be halved, sprinkled with honey or sugar and grilled. Grapefruit may be made into juice and served alone or with other fruit juices. It is also used to make marmalade.

Grapes

There are small seedless varieties and larger fruits containing seeds. They may be 'white' (or 'green') or 'black' (or 'red'). All fresh grapes should have a bloom on the skin and feel firm to touch. Don't buy soft or split fruits.

Usually eaten raw but may be added to sauces and some casseroles. To remove the skins from grapes, plunge in boiling water and boil for 1–2 minutes, drain and slip the skins off. Halve and remove the seeds before adding to sauce. White grapes are an essential ingredient in Véronique dishes. They may be squeezed and their juice served as a drink or made into wine.

Greengages

These are the size of small plums with yellow-green skins. Don't buy very hard fruit or damaged or blemished fruit.

Eat raw or cooked. Eat alone or incorporate in fruit salads or serve fresh or puréed and hot with cheese. They may be stewed and made into a wide variety of desserts or used in jam making.

Guavas

There are many different varieties which vary in size, shape and colour. All have a strong pungent aroma. The most common is round, up to 4 inches (10cm) across with a pink, fairly firm skin.

Eat raw or cooked. Cut a thin slice from each end and cut into quarters or smaller wedges. Eat the flesh and seeds. Peel if desired. May be stewed and used in desserts or made into jam or jelly.

Kiwi Fruit

These egg-shaped fruits have rough skins covered in very short hairs. They are ripe when slightly soft to the touch. Don't buy if soft or bruised. If only available hard, place in a fruit bowl with a selection of other fruits to hasten ripening.

Eat raw or cooked. The skin may be peeled and placed on top of meat to act as a tenderiser. Raw kiwi fruit are delicious on their own or may be incorporated in fruit salads, sweet and savoury. Puréed kiwi fruit may be used as the base for sorbets, fools etc. If making a kiwi fruit mousse, it is best to use agar-agar instead of gelatine as an enzyme in the kiwi fruit will gradually cause the gelatine to break down. They may also be used in chutney and jam making.

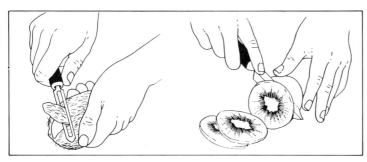

1. *Using a potato peeler, remove the rough brown skin.*
2. *Slice thinly and add to sweet or savoury dishes.*

Kumquats

These small oval fruits vary in size from ¾–2 inches (2–5cm) across. They should have a firm, bright, very slightly pitted orange skin which is shiny and unblemished. There are occasionally slight green patches which are not harmful. It is only the part of the fruit which hasn't faced the sun. They will gradually turn orange.

Eat raw or cooked. The whole of the fruit is eaten including the skin and seeds. Use whole or sliced in fruit salads, stewed and used in desserts or served in sauces as an accompaniment to meat or game. Halved kumquats may be served with fish. They may also be used in pickles, chutneys, marmalades etc. but they are very expensive for this method of preservation.

Lemons

There are many different varieties, some with thick and others with thin skins, but all should be bright yellow. Don't buy wrinkled or soft lemons.

To extract the juice from citrus fruits, cut in half through their 'equator', not from top to bottom, and turn gently on a lemon squeezer.
To use a zester, hold the lemon (lime or orange) in one hand and gently pull the zester over the fruit towards you.

Widely used in sweet and savoury dishes. Also used to prevent the discolouration of some vegetables, for example, Jerusalem artichokes, and fruits, for example apples. The zest can be removed with either a grater or zester. This removes the yellow peel which contains the essential oils without the white pith. Due to their high pectin content, lemons are widely used in jam and jelly making. The juice is often mixed with other fruit juices to serve as a drink.

Limes

The two most common varieties are the green limes, about 2 inches (5cm) in size and the yellow-green limes, about 1½ inches (4cm) in size. Both turn yellower as they ripen. Limes are similar to lemons but rounder with a slightly smoother skin. Buy only firm, unblemished fruit.

Frequently used in place of lemon in recipes. When substituting lime for lemon, use only two thirds the amount of lemon specified. Remove the zest in the same way as for lemon. A useful tip for extracting the maximum juice is to warm the lime and roll it round, firmly pressing and squeezing, on a work surface.

Lychees

The fruit should have a rough but firm brown skin with a bright pink-red blush. Don't buy lychees with broken skins.

Eat raw or cooked. Peel off the skin and eat the flesh, not the stone. Incorporate in fresh fruit or savoury salads. Stew and serve with other fruits or add to chicken, duck or pork recipes. They may be pickled.

Mangos

Don't buy mangos which are hard and green. All varieties of mango are green when under ripe but the colour changes as they ripen. The most commonly available are either a red-orange colour or golden yellow-orange.

Eat raw or cooked. The simplest method of preparing a mango to eat raw is to cut lengthways down the broadside of the mango about ½ inch (1.25cm) away from the centre. Then cut through the other side, the same distance from the centre, so

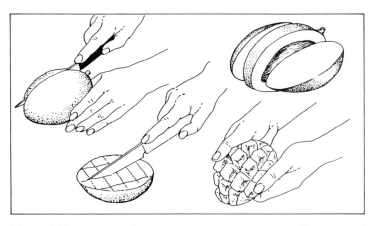

the long thin flat stone can be removed. Peel away the skin and cut off any flesh surrounding the stone. Make criss-cross cuts almost through to the skin of each half of mango, then turn the outer edge under so the middle of the fruit rises and cubes of flesh separate. Mangos can be incorporated in fruit or savoury salads, puréed and made into sorbets, fools etc. Hard mangos are used in chutneys.

MELONS

A ripe melon should have a firm skin but just 'give' when pressed at the ends. Some well known varieties are as follows:

Cut melons in half and scoop out all the seeds. Either cut into wedges and serve as an appetiser, or cut in small pieces, or use a teaspoon or melon baller to extract melon balls for use in sweet or savoury salads. If you wish to use the whole melon as a container for a salad, cut a slice from the top and cut out the flesh, scoop out the seeds then remove the remaining flesh. Ginger is often served with melon. The flesh may be puréed and mixed with other fruit juices to serve as a drink or cold soup.

Cantaloupe

Cantaloupe melons are almost round with either a green, grey-green or yellow rough skin. Don't buy if very hard or blemished with soft patches.

Charentais

Charentais melons are small and round with a pale grey-green skin.

Galia

Galia melons have rough green skins. They are round in shape.

Honeydew

Honeydew melons have either a dark green or bright yellow skin. They too are oval and have less flavour than other melons except when perfectly ripe.

Ogen

This round melon has a smooth, yellow-orange skin with faint green stripes.

Rock

This round melon has a coarse skin resembling netting.

Water

These large melons can weigh from 2½–20lb (1–9kg) but they usually weigh only a few pounds (kg). They can be round, oval or almost sausage shaped. The skin should look slightly waxy and be a deep green colour, sometimes with a

Water melons are eaten raw. The flesh varies in colour. It is usually bright red but may be yellow, and the combination of the two looks most attractive in salads. They can be incorporated in sweet or savoury salads. Unlike other melons,

yellow patch. When gently tapped, a ripe water melon should make a muffled noise, not sound hollow or soft.

the seeds are not in the centre of the fruit and are sometimes awkward to remove without breaking the flesh.

Nectarine

Similar in size to a peach but has a shiny, smooth yellow to red skin. Should be firm to the touch but 'give' slightly when pressed.

Eat raw or cooked. To remove the stone, cut round the nectarine, twist each half gently but firmly in opposite directions and scoop the stone out of one of the halves. May be stewed or preserved in jam making or chutneys.

ORANGES
Eating

There are many varieties of orange and orange hybrids (such as minneolas, topaz) on the market. The majority have bright orange skins but their sizes vary. An exception is the blood orange which has an orange skin flecked with red.

Peel before using and eat raw, squeeze and make the juice into a drink or sauce or add the segments to cooked dishes. The zest should be removed in the same way as the lemon zest, with a grater or zester, so only the bright orange zest with the volatile oils is obtained, not the bitter pith.

Seville

A bright orange-skinned fruit. Don't buy any fruits with soft patches.

The Seville orange is very bitter and primarily used to make marmalade, although it is also made into sauce to accompany savoury dishes. It is also used to make drinks and wine.

Ortanique

Similar in appearance to an orange but the skin is duller and marked.

Eat raw and include in fresh fruit and savoury salads. The fruit may be squeezed and the juice drunk on its own or mixed with other fruit juices.

Papaya

The ripe papaya should have a smooth green-yellow to orange skin with tiny freckle marks. Don't buy if firm and green or bruised with soft patches.

Usually eaten raw. Cut the fruit in half lengthways and scoop out and discard the slippery black seeds and connecting tissue. Eat with a spoon out of the skin or slice and add to fruit salads. Lemon or lime juices enhance its flavour. The juice may be used in drinks or poured over meat as it acts as a tenderiser.

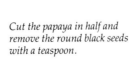

Cut the papaya in half and remove the round black seeds with a teaspoon.

Passion Fruit

The fruit is a dark purple-brown with a wrinkled appearance. This indicates that the fruit is ripe, not that it's going off.

Eat raw or cooked. Slice off the top and scoop out the flesh (the seeds are edible). Either use on its own, in fruit salads or desserts such as sorbets. It may also be used in jam making. The juice is used to make mixed fruit juices and punches.

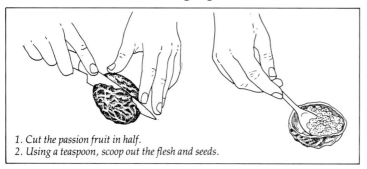

1. Cut the passion fruit in half.
2. Using a teaspoon, scoop out the flesh and seeds.

Peach

The round fruit has a yellow-red velvety skin. When ripe they bruise easily, so store carefully.

Eat raw or cooked. To remove the skin, plunge in boiling water for 1 minute, drain, place in cold water, then slip off the skins. Add to fruit or savoury salads, a variety of desserts and when squeezed, include in mixed fruit juices. May be used in preserves either as a chutney or jam.

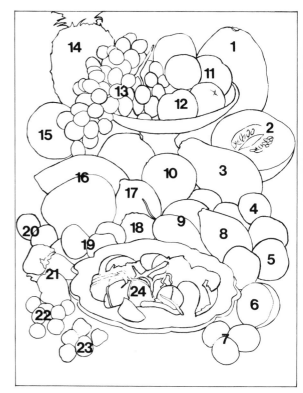

1   Pomelo
2   Melon, ogen
3   Papaya
4   Limes
5   Plums
6   Kiwi fruit
7   Kumquats
8   Prickly pear
9   Tamarillos
10   Pomegranates
11   Nectarines
12   Clementines
13   Grapes
14   Pineapple
15   Orange
16   Mangos
17   Lemon
18   Passion fruit
19   Apricots
20   Lychees
21   Strawberries
22   Blueberries
23   Raspberries
24   Exotic fruit salad

Pear	There are a wide variety of pears suitable for eating and cooking. Their shape and colour depends on the variety, but always make sure the skin is undamaged.	Eat raw, alone or in fruit or savoury salads, or stewed. To prevent discolouration, as soon as the fruit is peeled turn in lemon juice or, if preparing a large quantity of pears, cover with cold water with about 2 tablespoons of lemon juice. Pears are also used in chutneys.
Persimmon	The fruit should be about the size of a large tomato with a shiny, almost leathery yellow-orange skin. They should be slightly soft to the touch but the skin should not be split.	Eat raw or cooked. Add to savoury and sweet salads (the skin may be eaten). Puréed they can be made into sorbets, stewed they are used to make pies etc. At present they tend to be expensive but may be used to make jam, jelly or chutney.
Pineapple	The colour depends on the variety. Some pineapples remain green when ripe and others turn a golden yellow colour. To check a pineapple is ripe, pull a leaf. It should come off easily. Over-ripe fruit tends to 'weep', so look out for wet patches.	Eat raw, alone or in fruit or savoury salads, or cooked in desserts or savoury dishes. To prepare, cut off the leaves and base and gradually peel off the skin with a serrated knife. Slice or cut in wedges and remove the hard central core.
Plums	There are many different varieties of plums. Some are suitable only for cooking, others for eating and cooking. The colour varies from yellow to deep crimson. Don't buy soft or blemished fruit.	Victorias are one of the most well known plums, suitable for eating raw and adding to fruit salads. All plums may be stewed, added to numerous desserts and made into jam.
Pomegranate	The fruit is about the size of a large orange with a hard golden-red skin.	Usually eaten raw although occasionally the juice is added to meat dishes. To prepare, cut the fruit in half and scoop out the pulp and edible seeds. Squeeze the pulp through a sieve to extract the fruit juice.
Pomelo	The thick rinded citrus fruit is similar to a very large grapefruit but tends to be thinner and flatter at the ends. Its colour is either yellow or tinged green.	Usually eaten raw, it can be peeled very easily and divided into segments. As the membranes are fairly tough, it's worthwhile removing them by slitting the inner part of each segment with a knife and pulling the membrane back. The flesh is either pale yellow or pink. It can be used in sweet or savoury dishes or made into marmalade.

Prickly Pear	A ripe prickly pear is an orange or pinky orange colour, oval shaped with tufts of tiny bristles in spots forming diagonal lines across the skin. They are very sharp so be careful when testing. Press carefully; they should feel just soft.	Usually eaten raw with lemon, orange or lime juice sprinkled over, or included in fruit salads. They can be made into jellies or jams.
Quince	The shape varies from almost round to pear-shaped. They are hard and yellow in colour.	In this country quinces are usually only used in jam and jelly making because of their high pectin content, but one quince in an apple crumble or pie tastes very good. Abroad, quinces are far more widely used in sweet and savoury dishes.
Rhubarb	Choose rhubarb which is firm and pink and avoid green stems which are thick and fibrous. Look for fresh looking green leaves on the stalks.	Only eaten cooked. Remove the leaf and the base of each stem, cut into pieces and stew. Used mainly in sweet dishes but may be served puréed as a sauce with mackerel.
Tangerine	A small type of orange with a bright orange skin. Slightly pointed at the stem end.	Usually eaten raw but may be included in marmalades. The segments may be added to fruit or savoury salads or added to a variety of puddings.
Tamarillo	The skin is a red-brown colour and the fruit about the size of a large egg. The test for ripeness is to gently press a firm fruit. It should yield slightly to pressure.	Eat raw or cooked. Peel and cut into slices or chunks before adding to fruit or savoury salads. Puréed they can be served as a topping or base for other desserts. They may also be baked or grilled with meat or made into jam or chutney but they tend to be rather expensive for this.
Ugli	This cross between a tangerine and a grapefruit resembles them both. It is the size of a grapefruit but slightly pointed at the stem end. The thick skin is bumpy and a mottled green and orange-yellow colour.	Eat raw or cooked in the same way as a grapefruit or pomelo.

SAVOURY FRUIT SALAD
Serves 2 (265 Calories per serving)

Pineapple and ham is a well known combination, but the addition of papaya and Lymeswold cheese, tossed in a sweet and sour dressing, makes this an unusual meal.

4oz (120g) fresh pineapple
½ papaya, seeded and peeled
2oz (60g) cooked ham
2oz (60g) Lymeswold or any other strongly flavoured cheese
For the dressing
2 teaspoons olive oil
2 teaspoons lemon juice
1 teaspoon soy sauce
1 teaspoon caster sugar
endive or shredded lettuce to serve

① Cut the pineapple, papaya, ham and Lymeswold into ½-inch (1.25-cm) cubes, place in a bowl.

② Place all the dressing ingredients in a small bowl and whisk together or in a screw-top jar and shake well.

③ Pour the dressing over the salad and toss to mix.

④ Arrange the endive or lettuce on the serving plate and pile the salad in the centre.

> *Exchanges per serving:*
> Fat 1
> Fruit 1
> Protein 2
> Vegetable ½
> 10 Calories Optional Exchange

PARMA PAPAYA
Serves 2 (95 Calories per serving)

Parma ham is frequently served with melon. This alternative version combines papaya and lime with the strong flavour of Parma ham.

I papaya
lime juice
2oz (60g) thinly sliced Parma ham, fat removed
slices of lime to garnish

① Cut the papaya in half, remove and discard the black seeds, peel and cut each half into four wedges, cutting lengthways.

② Squeeze each wedge of papaya liberally with lime juice.

③ Wrap each wedge in Parma ham, garnish with slices of lime.

Exchanges per serving:
Fruit I
Protein I

CRUNCHY APPLE SALAD
Serves 2 (175 Calories per serving)

Choose really crisp apples for this recipe and make sure you brush them with lemon juice as soon as they're prepared to prevent them browning.

6oz (180g) low-fat soft cheese or curd cheese
4 teaspoons chopped chives
2 tablespoons low-fat natural yogurt
2 dessert apples
2 teaspoons lemon juice

① Beat the low-fat soft cheese, chives and yogurt together.

② Remove the cores from the apples, cut in half so the hole left by the core is at the top and bottom. Scoop out the apple using a grapefruit knife leaving a thin layer supporting the skin.

③ Brush the insides of the apple with lemon juice. Finely chop the scooped out apple and toss in the lemon juice, making sure all the apple is coated.

④ Mix the chopped apple and lemon juice with the cheese mixture and pile back into the apple halves. Serve with a mixed salad and bread roll to make a complete meal.

> *Exchanges per serving:*
> Fruit 1
> Protein 1 ½
> 10 Calories Optional Exchange

KUMQUAT REFRESHER
Serves 2 (100 Calories per serving)

This is a very refreshing combination of fruits served in a syrup delicately flavoured with orange flower water, lemon zest and a hint of mint. Orange flower water is sold at most chemists.

1 tablespoon sugar
6 tablespoons water
thin strip of lemon zest
1 teaspoon orange flower water
sprig of mint
9 kumquats, halved through the centre, not lengthways
4oz (120g) fresh pineapple cubes

① Place the sugar, water and lemon zest in a small saucepan. Heat gently until the sugar has dissolved, then boil fiercely for 1 minute.

② Remove from the heat and stir in the orange flower water, mint, kumquats and pineapple. Leave to cool.

③ Remove the lemon zest before serving.

> *Exchanges per serving:*
> Fruit 2
> 30 Calories Optional Exchange

BLACKCURRANT FOOL
Serves 2 (150 Calories per serving)

Any strong-flavoured fruits may be used instead of blackcurrants. Vary the fool according to the season and try it with redcurrants, raspberries or blackberries.

10oz (300g) blackcurrants
1–2 tablespoons water
artificial sweetener to taste
For the custard
2 teaspoons cornflour
¼ pint (150ml) skimmed milk
1 egg, beaten
1 tablespoon sugar

① Place the blackcurrants and water in a saucepan, cover and simmer until cooked. Remove the lid from the saucepan and boil hard for 4–5 minutes to reduce the amount of liquid.

② Sieve the blackcurrants, sweeten to taste with an artificial sweetener and leave until cold.

③ Blend the cornflour to a paste with a little milk. Heat the rest of the milk until steaming, add the cornflour paste and boil for 1 minute, stirring all the time. Allow to cool a little then pour into the beaten egg, stirring all the time.

④ Strain the custard into the top part of a double saucepan or into a bowl resting over a saucepan of simmering water. Stir in the sugar and heat gently, stirring all the time, until the custard thickens and coats the back of the spoon. Cover and leave until cold.

⑤ Stir the blackcurrant purée into the cold custard, transfer to two serving dishes.

Exchanges per serving:
Fruit 1
Milk ¼
Protein ½
40 Calories Optional Exchange

GOOSEBERRY FOAM
Serves 2 (175 Calories per serving)

I prefer to sweeten this dessert with sugar but if you wish to cut the number of calories used in your Optional Exchange, substitute the sugar with artificial sweetener. This will reduce the number of calories in the Optional Exchange from 125 to 25 per serving. If elderflowers are in season, add two sprigs to the gooseberries and use to garnish the desserts.

10oz (300g) gooseberries, topped and tailed
2 tablespoons white wine
10 teaspoons sugar
2 teaspoons gelatine
2 tablespoons hot water
1 egg white
pinch of salt

① Place the gooseberries and white wine in a saucepan, heat gently until the fruit begins to soften, stir in the sugar. Cover the saucepan and simmer gently for about 15 minutes until cooked.

② Press the gooseberries and their cooking liquor through a sieve, leave the gooseberry purée to cool.

③ Sprinkle the gelatine over the hot water and stir. Stand the container in a saucepan of simmering water and leave until the gelatine has completely dissolved.

④ Stir a little of the gooseberry purée into the dissolved gelatine, then pour into the rest of the purée; leave until beginning to set.

⑤ Whisk the egg white and salt until peaking, fold into the setting purée. Divide between two serving glasses and chill until ready to serve.

Exchanges per serving:
Fruit 1
125 Calories Optional Exchange

EXOTIC FRUIT SALAD
Serves 2 (100 Calories per serving)

This tangy fruit salad leaves a refreshing aftertaste. It can be eaten on its own or served with low-fat natural yogurt or single cream, but remember to include their Exchanges into your menu plan.

2-inch (5-cm) stick of cinnamon
4 tablespoons water
I tablespoon caster sugar
½ orange, zest and juice
8 lychees, peeled
I kiwi fruit, peeled and sliced
I persimmon, cut into six or eight segments

① Place the cinnamon, water and sugar in a saucepan. Remove the orange zest with a zester and add to the saucepan. If you don't have a zester, remove the peel from the orange with a potato peeler, then cut into fine strips no thicker than a matchstick.

② Heat the water, sugar etc. gently until the sugar has dissolved.

Increase the heat and boil fiercely for 1 minute. Allow to cool.

③ Squeeze the juice from the orange and add to the cool syrup.

④ Place all the prepared fruits in a serving dish, pour over the syrup and leave to marinate for 1–2 hours before serving.

Exchanges per serving:
Fruit 1 ½
45 Calories Optional Exchange

BLACKBERRY AND APPLE PIE
Serves 2 (310 Calories per serving)

The strong flavour of the blackberries combines well with the apples to make a really tasty dessert.

For the pastry
1½oz (45g) plain flour
pinch of salt
4 teaspoons margarine
1–2 teaspoons cold water
For the filling
10oz (300g) cooking apples, peeled, quartered, cored and sliced
3oz (90g) blackberries
3 tablespoons sugar

① Make the pastry as described on page 217. Cover and leave to rest in the cool while preparing the filling.

② Arrange half the apples and blackberries in a 1-pint (600-ml) pie dish, sprinkle with the sugar and cover with the remaining fruit.

③ Roll out the pastry a little larger than the pie dish, cut off a small strip to just cover the lip of the pie dish. Dampen the pie lip and press the strip of pastry onto the dish. Dampen the pastry edge with cold water and cover with the pastry top, press to seal.

④ Decorate the pastry edge with the prongs of a fork or by pressing the edge with a finger and using the back of the knife to cut through the join several times to form a seal. (A sweet pie does not generally have a fluted edge or a glazed top). Make a hole in the centre to release the steam while cooking.

⑤ Place on a baking sheet and bake at Gas Mark 6, 200°C, 400°F for 15 minutes, then reduce to Gas Mark 3, 170°C, 325°F for a further 20 minutes to cook the fruit.

Exchanges per serving:
Bread ¾
Fat 2
Fruit 1½
90 Calories Optional Exchange

ST CLEMENT'S SORBET
Serves 2 (190 Calories per serving)

According to tradition, a sorbet is served before a roast in order to clear the palate but it is more usual to serve one nowadays as a dessert. This is a particularly refreshing sorbet and looks attractive garnished with kumquats or kiwi fruit.

1 medium orange, zest and juice
1 lemon, zest and juice
4fl oz (120ml) water
4 tablespoons sugar
1 egg white
pinch of salt
1 kiwi fruit or 3 kumquats, sliced to garnish

① Remove the zest from the orange and lemon with a potato peeler, place in a small saucepan with the water and sugar.

② Dissolve the sugar in the water over a low heat, stirring occasionally. Bring to the boil and boil gently for 10 minutes. Leave to cool.

③ Squeeze the juice from the orange and lemon into a freezerproof container. Strain the syrup into the fruit juices. Cover, seal and freeze until a 'slushy' consistency is obtained. This will take about 1½–2 hours.

④ Whisk the egg white with the pinch of salt until peaking, fold into the half-frozen fruit syrup using a metal spoon.

⑤ Return to the freezer and freeze until firm.

⑥ Spoon or scoop into glasses and serve immediately, garnished with the kiwi fruit or kumquats.

> *Exchanges per serving:*
> Fruit 1
> 130 Calories Optional Exchange

MARINATED FRUITS

Serves 2 (80 Calories per serving)

This colourful fruit salad makes an attractive dessert suitable for any occasion. Serve on its own, with low-fat natural yogurt or single cream.

5-oz (150-g) wedge of honeydew melon or ½ a cantaloupe or ogen melon
1 kiwi fruit, sliced
1 persimmon, cut in wedges
4 black grapes, halved and seeded
1 small passion fruit
1 tablespoon brandy

① Cut the melon into chunks or shape into balls using a melon baller or teaspoon.

② Mix together the melon, kiwi fruit, persimmon and grapes. Scoop out the pulp and seeds from the passion fruit and stir into the other fruits.

③ Sprinkle with brandy and leave 2–3 hours to marinate before serving.

> *Exchanges per serving:*
> Fruit 2
> 20 Calories Optional Exchange

BRANDIED APRICOTS FLAMBÉ

Serves 2 (115 Calories per serving)

This is a dessert for a special occasion – why not flambé the apricots at the table? The cooked apricots in the arrowroot sauce can be used on their own as a stuffing for pancakes (page 35), or the brandy may be added to the sauce.

8 apricots, halved and stoned
6 tablespoons water
4 teaspoons caster sugar
1 teaspoon arrowroot
2 tablespoons brandy

① Place the halved apricots and water in a saucepan and heat gently. When the apricots begin to soften, sprinkle in the sugar, cover and simmer over a very low heat until cooked but still whole.

② Drain the apricots, reserve the syrup, and place in a flameproof dish.

③ Blend the arrowroot with a little of the syrup to form a paste, mix with the remaining syrup and return to the heat. Bring to the boil, stirring all the time, pour the thickened syrup over the apricots.

④ Heat the apricots and syrup over a low heat. Warm the brandy.

⑤ Remove the apricots from the heat, pour over the brandy and ignite.

Exchanges per serving:
Fruit 2
80 Calories Optional Exchange

RHUBARB AND DATE MERINGUE
Serves 2 (190 Calories per serving)

The sharpness of the fruit base contrasts well with the sweet meringue topping. Use a 5-inch (12.5-cm) deep ovenproof dish so the meringue isn't too thin.

1lb (480g) rhubarb, cut in short lengths
grated zest of ½ an orange
1 tablespoon orange juice
5 dates, roughly chopped
artificial sweetener to taste
1 egg, separated
pinch of salt
3 tablespoons caster sugar

① Place the rhubarb, orange zest and juice and dates in a saucepan, cover and heat gently until the juice runs from the rhubarb.

② When the rhubarb is cooked, stir round with a wooden spoon to make into a purée, increase the heat and boil for a few minutes to reduce. Sweeten to taste and leave to cool for a few minutes.

③ Beat the egg yolk into the rhubarb and date base, pour into an ovenproof dish, about 5 inches (12.5cm) in diameter.

④ Whisk the egg white and salt until peaking, add 1 tablespoon caster sugar and whisk again until peaking, fold in the remaining sugar and pile on top of the fruit. Draw up to points with a fork.

⑤ Bake at Gas Mark 6, 200°C, 400°F for 8–10 minutes until browned.

> *Exchanges per serving:*
> Fruit 1
> Protein ½
> 110 Calories Optional Exchange

PINEAPPLE SANDWICH
Serves 2 (170 Calories per serving)

This unusual dessert makes a refreshing end to a meal. Serve with a knife and fork.

4 slices fresh pineapple
2oz (60g) curd cheese
2oz (60g) cottage cheese
2 teaspoons caster sugar
1 tablespoon desiccated coconut, toasted

① Remove the skin and core from each slice of pineapple.

② Mix together the curd and cottage cheeses, sugar and coconut.

③ Spread the cheese filling round two slices of pineapple, top with the other two slices and serve.

Exchanges per serving:

Fruit 1

Protein 1

35 Calories Optional Exchange

SPICED FRUIT COMPÔTE

Serves 2 (120 Calories per serving)

To save buying several packets of different dried fruits, look out for shops which allow you to help yourself, or for packets of mixed fruits. As dried fruit is so sweet there is no need for sugar in the syrup.

4oz (120g) mixture of dried fruits such as peaches, apricots, prunes, apples, pears
4fl oz (120ml) orange juice
2 whole cloves
2 green cardamoms, seeds removed and pods discarded
2-inch (5-cm) stick of cinnamon
zest and juice of ½ lemon

① Wash the dried fruit, place in a bowl and add the orange juice and spices.

② Remove the lemon zest with either a zester or grater, add to the fruits with the lemon juice. Leave to soak overnight.

③ The next day, if necessary, add 1–2 tablespoons water as older dried fruits absorb more liquid. Bring the fruits and spices to the boil, cover and reduce the heat as low as possible. Simmer gently 10–15 minutes until the fruit is cooked.

④ Transfer to a serving bowl and leave to cool or serve warm. Remove the cinnamon stick before serving.

> *Exchanges per serving:*
> Fruit 2½

Top: Peach Sundae (see page 188)
Bottom: Spiced Fruit Compôte

PEACH SUNDAE
Serves 2 (95 Calories per serving)

It's best to make this dessert when peaches are in season and sweet and juicy. Shredded coconut helps to make this into a pretty dish but it can be difficult to buy. Desiccated coconut tastes equally good.

2 peaches
5oz (150g) raspberries
1 teaspoon arrowroot
2½ teaspoons sugar
2 teaspoons shredded or desiccated coconut, toasted

① Pour boiling water over the peaches, leave for 1 minute, plunge into cold water then slip off the skins. Halve and remove the stones.

② Sieve the raspberries. Blend a little of the purée into the arrowroot. Stir the arrowroot into the rest of the purée, add the sugar and bring to the boil, stirring all the time. Boil for 1 minute, allow to cool.

③ Pour the raspberry sauce over the peaches and sprinkle over the toasted coconut.

Exchanges per serving:

Fruit 1½

40 Calories Optional Exchange

CHERRIES IN RED WINE
Serves 2 (110 Calories per serving)

Cherries are in season for such a short time I like to make the most of them. They are delicious in fresh fruit salads, but stewed in red wine they become even more of a treat.

8oz (240g) red cherries
5 tablespoons red wine
4 teaspoons caster sugar
1-inch (2.5-cm) cinnamon stick

① Remove the stalks and stones from the cherries. If you don't possess a cherry stoner, cut each cherry in half and remove the stone. Catch any juices which may drip from the fruit and add to the wine.

② As the cherries are prepared, drop into the red wine and sprinkle with the caster sugar.

③ Add the cinnamon and bring to the boil, cover, reduce the heat and simmer gently for 10–15 minutes.

④ Serve warm or cool. Remove the cinnamon before serving.

Exchanges per serving:
Fruit 1
80 Calories Optional Exchange

BAKED APPLES
Serves 2 (115 Calories per serving)

The amount of sugar required for this recipe varies considerably according to which apples are used. I tested the recipe with Bramleys, but other varieties may require one more teaspoon of brown sugar which would add an extra 10 Calories per person.

2 × 6-oz (180-g) cooking apples
1 oz (30g) raisins
2 teaspoons brown sugar
good pinch mixed spice
3 tablespoons water

① Wash the apples and remove the cores. Cut ½ an inch (1.25cm) off the bottom of each core and replace in the apple to prevent the filling falling out.

② Cut the skin round the centre of each apple and place in an ovenproof dish.

③ Mix the raisins, sugar and spice together and press into the centre of each apple.

④ Pour the water into the dish and bake at Gas Mark 4, 180°C, 350°F until the apples are cooked right through, 50–60 minutes.

Exchanges per serving:
Fruit 1 ½
20 Calories Optional Exchange

CRANBERRY CRUMBLE
Serves 2 (220 Calories per serving)

Fresh cranberries are only available from October to January, but when they are out of season, frozen ones can be bought in large supermarkets or freezer stores.

7oz (210g) cranberries
6 tablespoons orange juice
artificial sweetener to taste
For the crumble topping
1½oz (45g) flour
4 teaspoons margarine
2 teaspoons sugar
1 tablespoon desiccated coconut

① Place the cranberries in a saucepan, add the orange juice, cover and simmer for about 10 minutes until the cranberries are just cooked, sweeten to taste.

② Transfer the cranberries to a 1-pint (600-ml) deep ovenproof dish.

③ Sieve the flour into a bowl, rub the margarine into the flour until the mixture resembles fresh breadcrumbs. Stir in the sugar and coconut.

④ Sprinkle the crumble evenly over the cranberries and bake in a preheated oven, Gas Mark 5, 190°C, 375°F for about 20 minutes until beginning to brown.

Exchanges per serving:

Bread ¾

Fat 2

Fruit 1

40 Calories Optional Exchange

TROPICAL SNOW
Serves 2 (70 Calories per serving)

Make this dessert and serve immediately. If it's made too far in advance, the egg white foam will gradually collapse.

½ a medium mango, peeled
½ a medium banana, peeled
finely grated zest of ½ a lemon
2–3 teaspoons lemon juice
1 ½ teaspoons caster sugar
1 egg white
2 lemon slices for garnish

① Mash the mango, banana, lemon zest, lemon juice and sugar.

② Whisk the egg white in a bowl until peaking.

③ Add the fruit purée to the egg white and whisk again to form a foam. Pile the snow into two serving dishes and serve garnished with lemon slices.

Exchanges per serving:
Fruit 1
25 Calories Optional Exchange

BAKING

I have divided this chapter into three categories: Bread; Scones, Cakes and Biscuits; and Pastries. All of these require cooking in an oven by radiant heat and the convection of hot air. Fan ovens keep the temperature fairly constant, but conventional ovens have a greater range of temperature. The middle shelf should be the temperature at which the oven is set, the top shelf a little hotter and the bottom shelf a few degrees cooler.

The main ingredients used for baking are flour, fat, sugar, eggs, liquid and flavourings. Each ingredient has a particular function to perform and the quantity and method by which it is incorporated into the recipe affects the end result.

Flour: There are three main types of flour: strong bread flour which has a high gluten content and is important to ensure successful breads and some pastries; plain flour which is used in biscuit and cake making and some pastries, and self raising flour which is made by adding raising agents to plain flour. Occasionally cornflour is added to plain flour to give a more tender crumb, for example when making shortbread.

Fat: Vegetable oil and margarine which is high in polyunsaturates are the only fats recommended for baking in the Weight Watchers Food Plan. Fat adds richness to mixtures and helps to increase keeping qualities. When creamed with caster sugar, margarine holds air which acts as a raising agent. As margarines high in polyunsaturates are soft, it is worth remembering the tip given in the introduction – to measure teaspoons and tablespoons of margarine, pack, then label them and store in the freezer for use in

'rubbing in' methods. Although the margarine doesn't solidify, it becomes much firmer and therefore easier and quicker to rub in.

Sugar: This obviously sweetens a mixture but is also a main source of food for yeast when breadmaking, it helps to incorporate air into margarine in creamed cakes and gives a softer texture to all flour mixtures.

Eggs: These enrich all mixtures. In cakes they are important as a raising agent as they trap air in tiny bubbles. In yeast mixtures, eggs retard the growth of the yeast so the dough takes longer to rise.

Liquid: The liquid added to mixtures turns to steam during baking and helps them to rise. When added to flour, liquid strengthens the gluten, which is an advantage when making bread but a disadvantage when biscuit and cake making as it produces a much harder crumb.

Flavouring: A wide variety of flavours, natural and synthetic, can be added to bread, scones, biscuits, cakes and pastries. In general, essences make mixtures drier but the addition of fruit, orange and lemon zests tend to make slightly moister mixtures.

Bread

The aroma of bread baking has always conjured up a feeling of nostalgia in me. The smell of freshly made bread is in a class of its own.

I've always enjoyed baking, in particular breadmaking, and still gain the same sense of achievement I had as a schoolgirl. Mixing a few basic ingredients and following a simple procedure results in a delicious, fresh hot loaf, and for this reason I make no apology for starting this chapter with a basic bread recipe.

To achieve good results it is important to understand the basic breadmaking terms.

a) **Dried yeast** must be dissolved in slightly sweetened warm liquid and then left in a warm place until frothy.

b) **Salt**. A little is added to the strong bread flour to increase the strength of the dough so it is able to become more elastic and hold a good structure.

c) **Fat** is added to the flour, usually by rubbing in, to make the bread more palatable and improve its keeping qualities.

The frothy yeast liquid is added to the flour mixture and mixed to form a dough. Transfer the dough to a lightly floured work surface.

d) **Kneading**. This can be done in 2–3 minutes in a food processor or in a mixer with a dough attachment, or 10–15 minutes by hand. This strengthens the flour and distributes the yeast evenly throughout the dough.

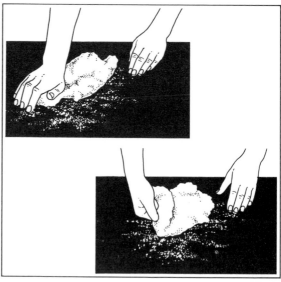

Using the palm of your hand, stretch the dough away from you. Using your knuckles, draw the dough back on top of itself. Repeat the process for 10–15 minutes.

e) **Rising**. The dough is covered with greased polythene and left to rise in a warm place. During this time the yeast, which is a living organism, feeds on the dough increasing its bulk. This stage can be carried out in the cool or in a refrigerator but the process is very much slower and takes several hours.

f) **Knocking back**. The dough is kneaded again to redistribute the yeast and bring it back into contact with its food, the flour. This second kneading only takes 2–3 minutes.

g) **Proving**. The shaped dough is covered and left for its final rising time.

h) **Baking**. The risen dough is baked in a preheated oven, about Gas Mark 8, 230°C, 450°F, which will kill the yeast and cook the dough. Breads are cooked in the centre of the oven, rolls nearer the top. The baked bread should sound hollow when tapped on its base.

Scones, Cakes and Biscuits

Even when following a weight reducing diet it is possible to eat a limited number of scones, cakes and biscuits. As long as they are carefully incorporated into the day's menu and allowance is made for their ingredients they can be enjoyed in the same way as any other food.

It is essential to weigh and measure ingredients accurately to achieve optimum results. I find it advisable to line baking sheets and tins with non-stick baking parchment, which eliminates the necessity for greasing them and therefore reduces the amount of fat required in each recipe. It also ensures the scones, cakes or biscuits are easily removed from the paper and the tins are left cleaner, so washing up is quicker.

The four main methods of making cakes and biscuits are whisking, melting, rubbing-in and creaming.

The whisking method is used when a high proportion of eggs and sugar are

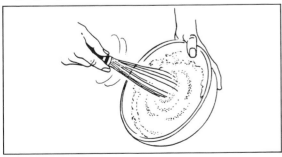

whisked together before folding in melted fat, if used, and sieved flour.

The melting method is used for some biscuits and occasionally cakes when fat,

syrup and sugar are melted together. These are usually very rich recipes and not suitable for the weight conscious.

The rubbing-in method is used in all three categories of baking. Margarine is rubbed into the flour by using only the tips of the fingers and thumbs as these are the coolest parts of the hand and help to prevent warming the fat. This method is

only suitable for recipes with up to half the amount of fat to flour.

The creaming method is widely used in cake and biscuit making. The margarine and sugar are beaten together until light and fluffy before gradually adding the eggs

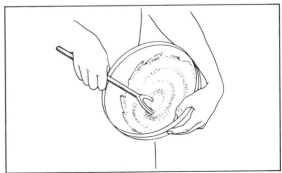

etc. This method is only used when there is half or more fat to flour.

Pastries

It's not suitable to include flaky, puff, rough puff, shortcrust, suet and filo pastries in your diet when trying to lose weight as they include too much fat and carbohydrate. However, it is possible to make a pseudo shortcrust pastry which can be used instead so you can include pies, flans etc. in your diet which can be eaten by the whole family.

Choux pastry is also included in this chapter as it is possible to make delicious desserts and savouries without adding too much fat and calories. And the pastry can be filled with delicious fruits and cheeses instead of the traditional rich fillings which will add unwanted Calories.

Self raising flour is rarely used in pastry making. Ordinary plain flour can be used for shortcrust and choux mixtures but the stronger bread flour gives a slightly better, crisper result in choux pastry which requires a more elastic dough.

SIMPLE PIZZA
Serves 4 (240 Calories per serving)

The amount of cheese, anchovy fillets and olives may be altered to suit individual tastes but don't be tempted to add salt as the anchovy fillets and olives supply ample salt to the topping.

2 teaspoons olive oil
4 tablespoons warm water
1 ½ teaspoons dried yeast
½ teaspoon sugar
4oz (120g) strong plain bread flour
½ teaspoon salt
2 teaspoons margarine
6oz (180g) onions, sliced
12oz (360g) tomatoes, skinned and roughly chopped
½ teaspoon oregano
pepper
3oz (90g) Mozzarella cheese, thinly sliced
1oz (30g) drained canned anchovy fillets, cut in half lengthways
5 black olives, stoned and halved

① Use a little of the olive oil to grease a sheet of polythene. Line a baking sheet with non-stick baking parchment.

② Measure the warm water into a bowl, dissolve the sugar in the water, add the yeast and stir until dissolved. Leave in a warm place for 10–15 minutes or until frothy.

③ Reserve 2 teaspoons flour. Sieve the remaining flour and salt together into a bowl, rub in the margarine.

④ Add the yeast liquid to the flour and mix to form a firm dough, add a little extra warm water if necessary.

⑤ Use the reserved flour to dust the work surface. Knead the dough until smooth and elastic. (If you have a food processor or mixer with a dough attachment, this can be achieved in 2–3 minutes, but it may be too small a quantity for large models.)

⑥ Place the dough in a clean bowl, cover with the sheet of oiled polythene and leave in a warm place until the dough has doubled in size.

⑦ Meanwhile, prepare the topping. Heat the remaining olive oil in a saucepan, add the onions and stir-fry for about 4 minutes until soft. Add the tomatoes and bring to the boil, reduce to a thick pulp, stirring from time to time. Allow to cool a little.

⑧ Turn the dough out and 'knock back'. Place on the prepared baking sheet, shape into an 8-inch (20-cm) circle with a slightly raised edge. Spread the tomato and onion mixture on top leaving an edge of about ½ inch (1.25cm) clear. Sprinkle with the oregano and pepper and leave in a warm place for 10–15 minutes.

⑨ Transfer to the oven and bake at Gas Mark 8, 230°C, 450°F for 15 minutes. Lift out of the oven and arrange the cheese, anchovy fillets and olives on top. Return to the oven for a further 15 minutes.

Exchanges per serving:

Bread 1

Fat 1

Protein 1

Vegetable 1 ½

10 Calories Optional Exchange

BASIC BREAD LOAF
Makes 1 large or 2 small loaves (2540 Calories per large loaf)

This recipe can be used to make white, granary or wholemeal bread and it can easily be adapted to shape into a plait or cottage loaf. To make a savoury loaf to serve with soups, add 3–4 tablespoons of freshly chopped mixed herbs to the flour.

1 teaspoon sugar
¾ pint (450ml) warm water
1 tablespoon dried yeast
1½lbs (720g) strong wholemeal, granary or plain bread flour
2 teaspoons salt
1 tablespoon margarine
1 teaspoon oil

① Dissolve the sugar in the water, add the yeast and stir until dissolved. Leave in a warm place for 10–15 minutes or until frothy.

② Reserve a tablespoon of flour. Stir the remaining flour and salt together in a bowl, rub in the margarine.

③ Add the yeast liquid to the flour and mix to form a firm dough, add a little extra warm water if necessary.

④ Use the reserved flour to lightly dust the work surface. Knead the dough on the floured surface for about 10 minutes until smooth and elastic. (If you have a food processor or mixer with a dough attachment, this can be achieved in 2–3 minutes.)

⑤ Place the dough in a clean bowl, lightly oil a sheet of polythene and use to cover the dough. Leave in a warm place until the dough has doubled in size. Meanwhile, use the remaining oil to grease a 2-lb (1-kg) loaf tin or two 1-lb (500-g) loaf tins.

⑥ Turn the dough out and 'knock back' for 2–3 minutes. Shape to fit the prepared tin or tins, cover with the oiled polythene and leave in the warm to prove. The dough should rise to the top of the tin and when lightly pressed with a finger should spring back.

⑦ Bake in a preheated oven, Gas Mark 8, 230°C, 450°F allowing about 30 minutes for the smaller loaves and about 35 minutes for the large loaf.

⑧ Turn the bread out of the tin and tap the base – it should sound hollow when cooked. Leave to cool on a wire rack.

Exchanges:

Use as for ordinary Bread Exchanges i.e. 1-oz (30-g) slice = 1 Bread Exchange.

Top: *Fruit Buns (see page 202)*
Basic Bread Loaf
Centre: *Granary Knots (see page 201)*
Bottom: *Sultana Cakes (see page 208)*

BRIOCHE
Serves 10 (145 Calories per serving)

These small individual brioche are delicious served warm for breakfast. Alternatively, the tops can be pulled off, some of the inside scooped out, and a savoury filling added for a snack lunch.

1 teaspoon oil
1 tablespoon sugar
4 tablespoons warm water
1 ½ teaspoons dried yeast
10oz (300g) strong plain bread flour
¼ teaspoon salt
5 teaspoons margarine
2 eggs, beaten
2 teaspoons skimmed milk

① Brush ten individual brioche tins with oil and grease a sheet of polythene.

② Dissolve ½ teaspoon sugar in the warm water, add the yeast, stir until dissolved. Leave in a warm place for 10–15 minutes until frothy.

③ Reserve a tablespoon of flour. Sieve the remaining flour and salt into a bowl, stir in the sugar and rub in the margarine.

④ Add the yeast liquid and sufficient beaten egg to mix to form a firm dough.

⑤ Use the reserved flour to lightly dust the work surface. Knead the dough on the floured surface for about 10 minutes until smooth and elastic (if you have a food processor or mixer with a dough attachment, this can be achieved in 2–3 minutes).

⑥ Place the dough in a clean bowl, cover with the polythene and leave in a warm place until the dough has doubled in size. This will take longer than a plain bread dough as it is much richer.

⑦ Turn the dough out and 'knock back' for 2–3 minutes.

⑧ Divide the dough into ten pieces. Use three-quarters of each piece to roll into a ball and place in the brioche tin. Use a little water to dampen the centre of the ball. Roll the remaining piece of dough into a smaller ball and press firmly on top of the first. Continue for all ten brioches.

⑨ Cover with polythene and leave to prove in a warm place for about 30 minutes. Brush with the milk mixed with any egg that may be over.

⑩ Bake at Gas Mark 8, 230°C, 450°F for about 15 minutes. Cool on a wire rack.

> *Exchanges per serving:*
> Bread 1
> Fat ½
> 25 Calories Optional Exchange

GRANARY KNOTS
Serves 9 (155 Calories per serving)

Although this recipe describes how to shape lengths of dough in knot-shaped rolls, other shapes such as twists, Catherine wheels, plaits or 'S' shapes can also be made. With other shapes it is best to dampen the end of the dough with a little water and press to the main shape. If desired, brush with egg or milk before baking, but remember to add the Exchanges.

½ teaspoon vegetable oil
7fl oz (210ml) warm skimmed milk
1 teaspoon sugar
2 teaspoons dried yeast
12oz (360g) granary bread flour
1 teaspoon salt
1 tablespoon margarine

① Line a baking sheet with non-stick baking parchment. Brush a piece of polythene with the oil.

② Place the warm milk in a jug, dissolve the sugar in the milk, then add the yeast and stir until dissolved. Leave in a warm place for 10–15 minutes or until frothy.

③ Reserve a tablespoon of flour. Stir the remaining flour and salt together in a bowl, rub in the margarine.

④ Add the yeast liquid to the flour and mix to form a firm dough.

⑤ Use the reserved flour to lightly dust the work surface. Knead the dough on the floured surface for about 10 minutes until smooth and

elastic. (If you have a food processor or mixer with a dough attachment, this can be achieved in 2–3 minutes).

⑥ Place the dough in a clean bowl, cover with the oiled polythene and leave in a warm place until the dough has doubled in size.

⑦ Turn the dough out and 'knock back' for 2–3 minutes. Divide into 9 pieces and roll each piece into a long length, tie loosely into a knot and place on the lined baking sheet. Cover with the oiled polythene and leave to prove until almost double in size.

⑧ Bake at Gas Mark 8, 230°C, 450°F for about 15 minutes. Leave to cool on a wire rack.

Exchanges:
Use as for ordinary Bread Exchanges i.e. 1-oz (30-g) slice = 1 Bread Exchange

FRUIT BUNS
Serves 12 (225 Calories per serving)

These fruit buns can easily be made into spicy hot cross buns. Add an extra ½ teaspoon mixed spice then, just before baking, mark the top of each bun with a cross using a very sharp knife. Alternatively, make the crosses out of pastry and add the exchanges to those given below.

¼ pint (150ml) skimmed milk
4 tablespoons water
2 tablespoons caster sugar
1 tablespoon dried yeast
1lb (480g) strong bread flour
1 ½ teaspoons salt
1 teaspoon mixed spice
4 tablespoons margarine
4oz (120g) mixed dried fruit
1 egg, beaten
For the glaze
4 teaspoons sugar
3 tablespoons water

① Line two baking sheets with non-stick paper.

② Gently heat the milk and water until warm, dissolve 1 teaspoon caster sugar in the liquid, sprinkle in the yeast and mix well. Leave in a warm place for 10–15 minutes until frothy.

③ Reserve a tablespoon of flour. Sieve the flour, salt and spice into a bowl.

④ Grease a sheet of polythene with a little margarine. Rub the rest of the margarine into the flour. Stir in the dried fruit.

⑤ Pour the yeast liquid into the flour and mix to form a firm dough,

adding the beaten egg as necessary. Do not discard the remaining egg.

⑥ Use the reserved flour to lightly dust the work surface. Knead the dough on the floured surface for about 10 minutes until smooth and elastic. (If you have a food processor or mixer with a dough attachment, this can be achieved in 2–3 minutes.)

⑦ Place the dough in a clean bowl and cover with the greased polythene. Leave in a warm place until the dough has doubled in size.

⑧ Turn the dough out and 'knock back' for 2–3 minutes. Divide into 12 pieces, roll each into a ball and place well spaced out on the prepared baking sheets. Cover with the greased polythene and leave in the warm to prove. The buns should almost double in size.

⑨ Bake in a preheated oven, Gas Mark 8, 230°C, 450°F for about 15 minutes. Cool on a wire rack.

⑩ While the buns are cooking, make the sugar glaze. Place the sugar and water in a small saucepan, heat

gently until the sugar has dissolved, then increase the heat and boil fiercely for 1 minute. Brush the warm buns with the hot glaze.

Exchanges per bun:
Bread 1¼
Fat 1
Fruit ⅓
25 Calories Optional Exchange

FLAPJACK
Serves 16 (155 Calories per serving)

This recipe is rather moreish so I find it best to store all the biscuits in a tin out of temptation's way!

8 tablespoons margarine
9 tablespoons soft brown sugar
1 tablespoon golden syrup
8oz (240g) rolled oats
½ teaspoon ground allspice

① Line a 7-inch × 11-inch (18-cm × 28-cm) Swiss roll tin with non-stick baking parchment.

② Gently heat the margarine, sugar and syrup in a saucepan.

③ When the margarine has melted, stir in the oats and spice, mix well.

④ Transfer the mixture to the prepared tin and press down to level the surface.

⑤ Bake in a preheated oven, Gas Mark 5, 190°C, 375°F for 20–25 minutes until golden brown. Mark into 16 fingers and leave in the tin to cool.

Exchanges per serving:
Bread ½
Fat 1½
40 Calories Optional Exchange

SHORTBREAD BISCUITS
Serves 12 (75 Calories per serving)

I always keep a vanilla pod in a jar of caster sugar for using when cake and biscuit making. It eliminates the need for vanilla essence and imparts a delicate flavour to sauces and desserts as well.

4 tablespoons margarine
2 tablespoons caster sugar
few drops of vanilla essence
3oz (90g) plain flour

1. Line a baking sheet with non-stick baking parchment.

2. Cream the margarine and caster sugar together, add the vanilla essence.

3. Reserve 2 teaspoons flour. Stir the remaining flour into the creamed margarine to form a soft dough.

4. Sprinkle the reserved flour over the work surface and rolling pin. Roll out the dough to about ¼ inch (5mm) thick, cut into 12 biscuits using a 2½-inch (6.5-cm) cutter. Re-roll the trimmings as necessary.

5. Place the biscuits on the prepared tin and prick with a fork. Bake at Gas Mark 3, 160°C, 325°F for about 15 minutes until lightly browned. Cool on a wire rack.

Exchanges per serving:

Bread ¼

Fat 1

10 Calories Optional Exchange

GINGERNUTS
Serves 12 (85 Calories per serving)

These crunchy little biscuits are made using the melting method. When rolling into small balls and flattening before baking, don't try to smooth out the cracks, these are characteristic of the biscuits.

4oz (120g) self raising flour
2 teaspoons ground ginger
1/4 teaspoon ground cinnamon
1/2 teaspoon bicarbonate of soda
4 tablespoons margarine
1 tablespoon clear honey
2 tablespoons soft brown sugar

① Line a baking sheet with non-stick baking parchment.

② Sieve the flour, spices and bicarbonate of soda into a bowl.

③ Gently heat the margarine, honey and sugar until the margarine has melted and the sugar dissolved.

④ Pour the margarine etc. into the flour and mix well.

⑤ Divide into 12 and roll into small balls, place on the lined baking sheet and flatten with the palm of your hand.

⑥ Bake at Gas Mark 4, 180°C, 350°F for about 15 minutes. Cool on a wire rack.

Exchanges per serving:

Bread 1/4

Fat 1

25 Calories Optional Exchange

SPEEDY SANDWICH CAKE
Serves 12 (180 Calories per serving)

This simple recipe is ideal when the family announce they are going to call in and see you. In a matter of minutes the ingredients can be weighed out, beaten and the cake is ready for baking.

½ teaspoon vegetable oil
8 tablespoons margarine
8 tablespoons caster sugar
2 eggs
½ teaspoon grated lemon zest
4oz (120g) self raising flour
1 teaspoon baking powder
3 tablespoons raspberry or strawberry jam
½ teaspoon icing sugar

1. Oil two 6½-inch (16-cm) sandwich tins with the oil and line the bases with baking parchment.

2. Place the margarine, caster sugar, eggs and lemon zest into a bowl. Sieve in the flour and baking powder and beat all the ingredients together, using a wooden spoon, for about 1½ minutes.

3. Divide the mixture between the prepared tins, level the surfaces and bake in a preheated oven, Gas Mark 3–4, 170–180°C, 325–350°F for 25–30 minutes. Allow to cool for 2–3 minutes, then turn out onto a cooling rack and leave until cold.

4. Sandwich the cakes together with the jam and dust the top with the sieved icing sugar.

> *Exchanges per serving:*
> Bread ¼
> Fat 2
> 80 Calories Optional Exchange

Top: *Gingernuts (see page 205)*
Speedy Sandwich Cake
Centre: *Shortbread Biscuits (see page 204)*
Bottom: *Flapjacks (see page 203)*

SULTANA CAKES
Serves 10 (115 Calories per serving)

These small cakes are very easy to make. Try adding a little mixed spice or ginger to the flour.

4 tablespoons margarine
4 tablespoons caster sugar
1 egg, beaten
1½oz (45g) sultanas
2½oz (75g) self raising flour

① Arrange ten paper cake cases in a bun tin.

② Cream the margarine and sugar until light and fluffy, add the egg a teaspoon at a time, beat well after each addition.

③ Fold the sultanas into the creamed mixture, then sieve the flour and fold into the mixture using a metal spoon.

④ Divide the mixture between the cake cases and bake at Gas Mark 5, 190°C, 375°F for 15–20 minutes. Cool on a wire rack.

> *Exchanges per serving:*
> Bread ¼
> Fat 1
> 45 Calories Optional Exchange

BOIL-BAKE CAKE

Serves 14 (260 Calories per serving)

This is an adaptation of a recipe used by my grandmother and mother during the second world war when eggs were in short supply. It has more the consistency of a tea loaf than a fruit cake but remains a family favourite. Use a cake tin which has a 7-inch (17.5-cm) inside measurement.

14fl oz (420ml) water
10½oz (315g) mixed dried fruit
12 tablespoons caster sugar
7 tablespoons margarine
1 teaspoon mixed spice
14oz (420g) self raising flour
1 teaspoon bicarbonate of soda
pinch of salt

1. Line a 7-inch (17.5-cm) deep cake tin with non-stick baking parchment, leaving at least 1 inch (2.5 cm) of paper above the level of the tin.

2. Heat the water, mixed fruit, sugar, margarine and mixed spice gently, simmer for 10 minutes, stirring occasionally. Leave to cool.

3. Sieve the flour, bicarbonate of soda and salt into a bowl. Beat in the cool fruit mixture. Transfer to the prepared tin and bake immediately in a preheated oven, Gas Mark 4, 180°C, 350°F for 1 hour 30 minutes – 1 hour 40 minutes. Leave to cool for 5 minutes, then transfer to a cooling rack until cold. Cut into 14 slices.

Exchanges per serving:
Bread 1
Fat 1½
Fruit ¾
50 Calories Optional Exchange

LUXURY FRUIT RINGS
Serves 2 (300 Calories per serving)

It's hard to believe that you can be following a slimming diet and still enjoy a dessert like this one. It's important to make a slit in the choux pastry to allow the steam to escape or the pastry will be soggy.

For the choux pastry
3 tablespoons water
4 teaspoons margarine
1oz (30g) plain flour or strong white bread flour, sieved
1 egg, beaten
For the filling
1 kiwi fruit, sliced and halved
7½ tablespoons frozen dessert topping
5oz (150g) raspberries or halved strawberries
½ teaspoon icing sugar to dust the tops

① Line a baking sheet with non-stick baking parchment.

② Make the pastry. Gently heat the water and margarine in a saucepan until the margarine has melted. Increase the heat and bring to a rolling boil. Tip in all the flour and beat well over a moderate heat for 1 minute. By this time the mixture will be in a ball. Allow to cool a little and then gradually add the egg, beating well after each addition.

③ Using a ½-inch (1.25-cm) plain nozzle, pipe a 3-inch (7.5-cm) circle on the prepared baking sheet. Pipe another circle on top of the first. Repeat this procedure to form two rings.

④ Bake in a preheated oven, Gas Mark 6, 200°C, 400°F. Immediately the choux rings are in the oven, increase the heat to Gas Mark 7, 220°C, 425°F. Cook for 30 minutes until well risen and golden brown. Make a slit in each ring to allow the steam to escape. Return to the oven for a further 5 minutes. Cool on a wire rack.

⑤ No more than half an hour before serving, cut horizontally through each choux ring. Arrange the halved slices of kiwi fruit on the bottom ring, top with the frozen dessert topping and arrange the raspberries or strawberries on top. Cover with the top of the choux ring and dust with icing sugar. If there are any raspberries or strawberries over, pile them in the centre.

Exchanges per serving:
Bread ½
Fat 2
Fruit 1
Protein ½
70 Calories Optional Exchange

Luxury Fruit Rings

SAVOURY CHEESE PUFFS
Serves 2 (325 Calories per serving)

Fill these puffs just before serving so the pastry balls remain crisp. Use a hard cheese with a good strong flavour for the pastry.

For the choux pastry
3 tablespoons water
4 teaspoons margarine
1oz (30g) plain flour or strong white bread flour, sieved
½oz (15g) cheese, grated
1 egg, beaten
For the filling
4oz (120g) curd cheese
1oz (30g) smoked ham, finely chopped
1 tablespoon chopped chives
1 tablespoon chopped parsley
2 tablespoons low-fat natural yogurt
dash of chilli sauce
salt
sprinkling of cayenne to garnish

① Line a baking sheet with non-stick baking parchment.

② Make the pastry. Gently heat the water and margarine in a saucepan until the margarine has melted. Increase the heat and bring to a rolling boil. Tip in all the flour and beat well over a moderate heat for 1 minute. By this time the mixture will be in a ball. Allow to cool a little, then add the cheese and gradually add the egg, beating well after each addition.

③ Either spoon or pipe the choux pastry onto the prepared baking sheet to form 10 balls.

④ Bake in a preheated oven, Gas Mark 6, 200°C, 400°F. Immediately the balls are in the oven, increase the heat to Gas Mark 7, 220°C, 425°F. Cook for about 15 minutes until well risen and golden brown. Make a slit in each puff with a sharp knife to allow the steam to escape. Return to the oven for a further 5 minutes. Cool on a wire rack.

⑤ Prepare the filling. Mix together the curd cheese, ham, chives, parsley and yogurt. Season to taste with the chilli sauce and salt.

⑥ A short while before serving, spoon the filling into each cheese puff. Pile into a dish and dust with a sprinkling of cayenne pepper.

Exchanges per serving:
Bread ½
Fat 2
Protein 2
25 Calories Optional Exchange

SCONES
Serves 8 (145 Calories per serving)

Contrary to common belief, scones rise better if allowed to stand for about 20 minutes before placing in a very hot oven. If desired, 2oz (60g) sultanas may be added to the flour, which will add 15 Calories Optional Exchange per scone.

8oz (240g) plain flour
2½ teaspoons baking powder
¼ teaspoon salt
8 teaspoons margarine
¼ pint (150ml) skimmed milk

① Line a baking sheet with non-stick baking parchment.

② Reserve 2 teaspoons flour. Sieve the remaining flour, baking powder and salt into a bowl. Rub in the margarine until the mixture resembles fresh breadcrumbs.

③ Make a well in the centre of the flour, add most of the milk and mix to form a soft dough with a round-bladed knife. Add more milk as necessary.

④ Use the reserved flour to sprinkle over the rolling pin and working surface. Roll out the dough to ½–¾ inch (1.25–2cm) thick. Using a 2½-inch (6.25-cm) round cutter, cut into 8 scones and place on the lined tin. Leave to stand 15–20 minutes. Brush the tops with the remaining milk, if desired.

⑤ Bake in a preheated oven, Gas Mark 8, 230°C, 450°F for about 10 minutes. Cool on a wire rack.

Exchanges per scone:

Bread 1

Fat 1

5 Calories Optional Exchange

FILLED CHEESE SCONES

Serves 8 (275 Calories per serving)

I've used Cheddar cheese in the scone dough and the filling but it is worth changing the filling cheese to Lymeswold or Double Gloucester to add variety.

For the scones
8oz (240g) plain flour
2½ teaspoons baking powder
¼ teaspoon salt
½ teaspoon powdered mustard
8 teaspoons margarine
3oz (90g) Cheddar cheese, finely grated
¼ pint (150ml) + 1 teaspoon skimmed milk
For the filling
8oz (240g) low-fat soft cheese
3oz (90g) Cheddar cheese, grated
dash of chilli sauce
few lettuce leaves
2 tomatoes, sliced
few slices cucumber

(1) Line a baking sheet with non-stick baking parchment.

(2) Reserve 2 teaspoons flour. Sieve the remaining flour, baking powder, salt and mustard into a bowl. Rub in the margarine until the mixture resembles fresh breadcrumbs. Stir in the grated cheese.

(3) Make a well in the centre of the flour, add most of the milk and mix to form a soft dough with a round bladed knife. Add more milk as necessary.

(4) Sprinkle the work surface with the reserved flour and lightly dust the rolling pin. Roll out the dough to form a ¾-inch (2-cm) circle.

(5) Transfer the scone to the lined baking sheet, brush with the teaspoon of milk and mark into eight wedges. Leave to stand 15–20 minutes.

(6) Bake in a preheated oven at Gas Mark 8, 230°C, 450°F for 15–20 minutes until well risen, golden and cooked through. Cool on a wire rack.

(7) While the scones are cooling, mix together the cheeses and season with chilli sauce.

(8) Cut the scones in half horizontally. Spread the cheese filling over each half. Arrange the lettuce, tomato and cucumber on the bottom half, replace the top and cut into eight portions.

Exchanges per serving:
Bread 1
Fat 1
Protein 1¼
Vegetable ⅓
10 Calories Optional Exchange

Filled Cheese Scones

ROCK BUNS
Serves 12 (160 Calories per serving)

The name of these cakes refers to their shape, not their texture! Use demerara, granulated or caster sugar, whichever you prefer.

8oz (240g) plain flour
2½ teaspoons baking powder
¼ teaspoon salt
¼ teaspoon ground cinnamon
good pinch grated nutmeg
5 tablespoons sugar
5 tablespoons margarine
2oz (60g) dried fruit
1 egg, beaten
approximately 4 tablespoons water

① Line a large baking sheet with non-stick baking parchment.

② Sieve the flour, baking powder, salt and spices into a bowl. Stir in the sugar.

③ Rub in the margarine until evenly distributed throughout the flour. Stir in the dried fruit.

④ Make a well in the centre of the flour etc. Pour in the egg and 2 tablespoons water. Mix to form a firm dough adding additional water as required.

⑤ Shape the mixture into 12 mounds on the prepared baking sheet, rough up the edges with a fork to form a rock shape. Bake in a preheated oven, Gas Mark 6, 200°C, 400°F for about 20 minutes until risen and brown. Cool on a wire rack.

> Exchanges per serving:
> Bread ½
> Fat 1
> 70 Calories Optional Exchange

SHORTCRUST PASTRY
Serves 2 (155 Calories per serving)

This recipe is used in a number of savoury and sweet recipes throughout the book. Two recipes, one for a sardine quiche and one for fruit tarts, are given in this section, but the guidelines given below should always be followed whatever the recipe.

1½oz (45g) plain flour
pinch of salt
4 teaspoons margarine
1–2 teaspoons ice-cold water

① Sieve the flour and salt into a small bowl. Reserve 2 teaspoons.

② Add the margarine, if possible margarine which has been stored in the freezer. Rub into the flour using the tips of your fingers and thumbs.

③ Mix the cold water into the pastry with a round-bladed knife. If time allows, wrap in foil or clingfilm and refrigerate for 15–20 minutes.

④ Dust the work surface and rolling pin with the reserved flour. Roll out the pastry using short, light movements away from you. Turn the pastry to roll to the correct shape. Don't alter the movement of the rolling as this will stretch the pastry and cause it to shrink during cooking.

⑤ Bake according to the recipe, usually between Gas Mark 5–6, 190–200°C, 375–400°F for the first 15 minutes. If using the pastry for flans or pastry bases, it is worth standing the pie or flan plate on a baking sheet which has been heated in the oven. This helps the pastry to bake evenly and not become 'soggy' on the bottom.

> *Exchanges per serving:*
> Bread ¾
> Fat 2

FRUIT TARTS
Serves 2 (220 Calories per serving)

Almost any fruit can be served in this way and, as a treat, they can be enjoyed with single cream or whipped dessert topping.

For the pastry
1 ½oz (45g) plain flour
pinch of salt
4 teaspoons margarine
1–2 teaspoons cold water
For the filling
2 medium apricots, stoned and cut into wedges or 2 medium dessert plums, stoned and cut into wedges or 5oz (150g) strawberries, halved
For the glaze
1 teaspoon arrowroot
5 tablespoons fresh orange juice
1 teaspoon sugar

① Make the pastry as described on page 217.

② Roll out and line two 3½-inch (9-cm) fluted flan cases. Prick the pastry bases. Cut two circles of non-stick baking parchment a little larger than the flan cases. Place each circle of paper in the pastry case and weigh down with a few dried beans. Transfer to a hot baking sheet and bake at Gas Mark 6, 200°C, 400°F for 10 minutes, remove the paper and beans and return to the oven for a further 4–5 minutes. Leave to cool.

③ Arrange the prepared fruit in the pastry cases.

④ Make the glaze. Blend the arrowroot to a paste with a little of the orange juice. Pour the orange juice, arrowroot and sugar into a very small saucepan. Bring to the boil, stirring all the time. Boil for 1 minute.

⑤ Brush the glaze over the fruit.

> *Exchanges per serving:*
> Bread ¾
> Fat 2
> Fruit ½
> 30 Calories Optional Exchange

Fruit Tarts

INDEX